The Weight and Wealth Factors™

Parallel Factors
for Weight Management
and Wealth Accumulation

Written by Angie Hollerich, CEP, CCA
with Mary Zeitler, MA Ed., CGFI

Acknowledgments

This book is dedicated to my husband and best friend Jack, for all his support and encouragement, but most of all for his unconditional love, to my children Kari and Greg, for their patience, understanding and love, to Mary for all of her help, knowledge and support, to Denise for her wonderful graphics, illustrations and help in putting this book and the recipe cards together.

Contents

Introduction

For the past ten years I have successfully taught my clients the strategies for financial planning and wealth accumulation. This has been accomplished by addressing the factors that affected their ability to succeed: understanding the relationship between what goes on in their head and their actual life experiences, and their ability to apply the strategies necessary before they can move forward with their plan.

Using individual consulting, workshops, presentations and seminars, I have helped individuals learn to address those factors, set their goals, develop a positive attitude, and evaluate their feelings related to money.

I have not been as fortunate in my battle of the bulge. For more years than I would like to admit, I had been unsuccessful in controlling my weight: a series of fad diets, starvation diets, and on, and on, and on! The yo-yo weight loss and gain seemed to be my destiny. I could not achieve weight management.

At age 51, I was part of the 55 percent (now in 2003 65 percent) of the adults in the United States that were overweight; the one person out of six that was obese. I took a good look at myself and knew I wanted to take control; so I started on that roller coaster ride yet again. I attempted to lose the 60 pounds that I managed to put on over the last ten years. This time I sat down and took a good look at the options available, wrote down my short-, intermediate-, and long-term goals and objectives, and researched the factors that seemed to affect my ability to be successful. While educating myself I said, "WAIT A MINUTE!" Aren't those the same factors that have made my financial clients successful with their finances?"

When I applied the same paralleled factors to my weight management program, great things started to happen. Once I addressed the factors, I knew it was not what I ate, but mastering the factors that would lead to my successful weight management.

Here is a list of the factors:
Environment, Motivation, Attitude, Habits, Family, Budget, Education, Goals, Time, Age, Needs versus Wants, and Risk.

This book identifies the above factors and breaks them into both areas of weight and wealth. Exploring these factors will help identify the "stuff" that may be limiting your success in weight management and wealth accumulation.

I decided to free myself of all the "stuff" out there and simply apply my wealth factors to my weight management program. It worked! I've lost 65 lbs. I went from a size 18-20 to a size 10-12. I have kept the weight off for 12 months and counting.

Today will always be "The first day of the rest of my life," because I have made a life change, not a food change. I knew I finally had the control I needed with my weight and wealth! I was encouraged by my friends to share my story and my solution by writing this book and recipe boxes. During the process I realized I needed help.

I knew how I managed my weight issues, but I had to broaden the information. My ability to reach all the individuals with weight issues that differed from mine was limited. When sharing my dream with my very good friend, Mary Zeitler, (who has been involved with group fitness for the past 19 years) she offered to help me with the weight factors and strategies. Thanks to Mary, the information written in the weight portion of the book and recipe cards addresses strategies that will guide you to successful weight management. I could not have accomplished this without Mary's support, knowledge, and assistance.

Why is this book so important? Open a magazine, read a newspaper, watch television, or listen to the radio. The top two concerns on America's mind are: 1) how to successfully manage weight, and 2) once the goal of a healthy, long life has been achieved, how to accumulate enough wealth to pay for those added years in retirement.

Unlike other books that will address these issues, this book offers the solutions. The frustration of continued efforts with no logical approach only results in negative results, or results that don't last. I can tell you from experience that the negative cycle does more damage then the excess weight or lack of sufficient financial funds. If we learn to approach these issues one factor at a time, we learn it doesn't have to be confusing or intimidating, and we do not have to be afraid or confused.

When you use a journal, you enable yourself the opportunity to track, address, and control the factors that influence your life. Lifelong accomplishments are available to all of the people out there who wonder why they are always struggling for Weight Management and Wealth Accumulation.

I believe in this product because I am living proof that it works. It can work for you, too.

To Your Health–To Your Wealth–To Your Quality of Life!!

Journal and

Visualization

*Journaling allows more of the totality
of what we are to come alive.*
G. F. Simons

Journal

What is journaling? We hear about it on the "Oprah" show, and from our friends. I think of it as letting my inner voice speak to me on many levels. When I was growing up, I kept a diary. A few minutes a day I wrote down my thoughts, feelings, and concerns. I kept the information to myself, maybe sharing it with close friends. I have found that writing things down has literally transformed my life. It is as simple as getting out a pen and paper. The good news is that there are no rules, and I don't know about you, but I hate rules. You can write what you want, how long you want, and can do whatever you want with the information.

What I hope you will do is use the journal, and reform your life with respect to how you manage your money and your weight. You will find that when you take the time to use your journal you will reveal the "hidden" agenda that keeps you from your potential successes.

Think
receiv
inner
nal at

Are yo
the hi
said h
you w

Be car

There

Journal and Visualization

As we begin to journal, our subconscio
insights that can help us make dec
make more sense of our past dec

If you've never had a jour
prepare mentally as we
a friend's support i
five minutes eve
wealth. Prep
following

Da

experiences; this is the subconscious, which most psychologists believe runs our lives. We truly don't know what we are doing.

That is why mental health experts agree that less than 10 percent of changing a behavior is willpower. Over 75 percent of our transformation is getting to the core of our subconscious issue, and believe me, if we can get to the hidden problem, and discover the real issue, the solution is much clearer.

Journaling can write your childhood wrongs.
Catherine L Taylor,
Author of The Inner Child
Workbook

---

us takes over, revealing
sions, calm our fears, and
sions.

al, as with any habit, it is helpful to
as physically. You may want to enlist
the beginning. Each of you can take just
ty day to write your thoughts on weight and
ration of any kind increases your likelihood of
through with your goal.

e your entries; even if you've just jotted a few lines, it will
get you started writing. The first words will seem the hardest.
Use your own technique, there is no one kind.

When you journal you can:
  — write down what's on your mind
  — answer the questions in your
    The Weight and Wealth Factors activities.

Write a letter to yourself, to a friend or to a family member.
Journaling is simple, but again, not always easy.

Get Out of the Way...
Accumulate pages, not judgements...
Leap, and the net will appear.
                                    Julie Cameron

Even though I say it's a simple process, most of us still balk at
the thought of it and rush to find excuses:

Barriers to Journaling:

1. Fear of doing it wrong: Since there is no right or wrong way to journal, you just can't do it wrong.

2. Having no time: Think of how much you are worth: are you worth 5 to 10 minutes a day? You will find if you take the time for important things, you will be successful.

3. Too much will come out: Yes, you may open Pandora's box, but not facing the facts will be much worse. Think of how limitless you will feel, once you set yourself free.

✎ Activity

If you have already used a journal, you have experienced the rewards. For those of you who need motivation, here are some ideas to help you get started.

1. Write down the good and bad ways you managed your weight and wealth that day.

2. Make a list of the things for which you are grateful, in relation to your weight and wealth.

3. "In a perfect world..."(Complete the phrase related to your weight and wealth).

4. Write 4-7 endings for each of the following statements:
   "I am..."
   "I realize..."
   "I will..."
   "I know..."
   "I want..."

5. Make a gratitude list.

6. Get out a picture of yourself, and write down what changes you would like to see.

7. Write down five qualities you admire in yourself.

8. Write down five qualities you don't admire in yourself.

9. Write down five qualities you admire in others.

10. Write down five qualities you don't admire in others.

11. Remember the last compliment you received.

12. Write down the last compliment you gave and to whom it was given.

13. Complete this phrase, I would be willing to change the following about me _____.

14. Is the truth important to you, even if it's not what you want to admit?

15. What bad wealth habits are you willing to change?

16. What good wealth habits would you be willing to share with others?

17. What bad health habits are you willing to change?

18. What good health habits would you be willing to share with others?

When you are finished, evaluate how you feel about journaling. Remember, your attitude will play an important part in your weight management and wealth accumulation.

> *Visualization is a good*
> *friend of mine.*
> *Anonymous*

Visualization

When asked how he accounted for his amazing inventive genius, Thomas Alva Edison replied, "It is because I never think in words; I think in pictures." Edison was a master at picturing in his mind the objects he desired to invent.

People who are able to visualize what they want have accomplished phenomenal achievements. Edison was told no light could exist in a vacuum, but he saw it and believed it could be done.

Other accomplished people see their success before it happens. Actor Jim Carrey wrote himself a check for a million dollars and put it in his wallet. His first big movie contract paid him a million dollars!

One of the most forceful methods for this is called visualization. We all have the power to see our family, friends, or homes without standing in front of them; this is visualization. Simply put, seeing with the mind's eye.

The whole concept can be used with regard to your weight management and wealth accumulation.

In her book, *The Joy of Visualization*, Valerie Wells says, "A picture is worth a thousand words, and visualizing is worth a thousand efforts." As far back as the 19th century B. C., Virgil said, "Mind moves matter."

These pictures will help you surpass all of your expectations and accomplishments. I know you're thinking, "Sure! See it and it will happen!" Well, it will, and the good news is that it only takes a few minutes a day. It's like daydreaming about how you would like things to be.

Just sit down, breathe deeply, close your eyes, and start dreaming about how things will be when you reach your goals. Visualization is not just seeing; it's smelling, feeling, and hearing the whole picture. The clearer you can make the image the better; your mind is like a computer; save the picture, call it back several times.

My wanting to be Mr. Universe came about because I saw myself so clearly, being up there on the stage and winning.
                                    Arnold Schwarzenegger

Have you ever been told to stop daydreaming? Don't ever let anyone tell you to stop your dreams. The key to successful visualization is to dance to the beat of a different drummer.

That can be done with your feet planted firmly to the ground. However, it will take commitment and the willingness to work hard until your have found your fulfillment.

If we take the time to look around us, everything we see was a figment of someone's imagination. Look at that picture on the wall, the house in which you are living, or the car you drive; someone had to have visualized it to make it happen. You will be using the same process.

Imagination sets the goal 'picture' which our automatic mechanism works on. We act, or fail to act, not because of 'will' as is so commonly believed, but because of imagination.

Maxwell Maltz

We should never run out of dreams. If we focus on our dreams and our goals for weight management and wealth accumulation, we will be more successful than we ever believed.

Use the support around you when nurturing your dreams; don't let anyone discourage you. You take control of your own destiny; you don't need that kind of negativity around you.

Now you are ready, set, go!!!!

"...You may be disappointed if you fail, but you are doomed if you do not try."

Beverly Sills

Factor 1

Environment

We are all wanderers on this earth.
Our hearts are full of wonder, and
our souls are deep with dreams.
                    Gypsy saying

Fac**1**or

Environment

Weight

You are watching TV. The ad for your favorite pizza cries out to you. WOW! That really looks good! The next thing you know, you have ordered a pizza and are eating it while you watch your favorite show! How did that happen? Everything around us, our environment, influences our ability to use good weight management skills. Just as with wealth, everything with which we come in contact influences our thoughts and subliminally influences many of our weight management decisions. Who wants to control the factors that influence our weight anyway? Most people want to enjoy what they eat! The trick is this: learn to eat what you enjoy, as well as eat what you need! Learning weight management may be hard work, but the benefits of life-long health and fitness are well worth it!

The highest reward for man's toil is not
what he gets for it, but what he becomes by it.
                    John Ruskin

With what do you surround yourself? The following factors not only influence us to buy certain food products, but also may influence our perceptions and attitudes about what is or is not healthy. This can result in a general misconception that only the "beautiful" people are healthy, fit people. It seems that this misconception is one held by many people in our society today.

- Billboards
- Advertising
- Television
- Radio

- Newspapers
- Magazines
- Floor displays in stores

✎ Activity

Use your journal and record all messages that you receive from the above categories (You may think of some of your own!) for one week. Write down not only the items that you were tempted to purchase to eat, but the emotions evoked by the messages. Also, write down how the message made you feel in relation to yourself.

Did you know that 65 percent of Americans are overweight and one in five is considered obese? The numbers are expected to increase due to obesity in children. So what can we do? It is easy to feel helpless and just give up, but do not do that! As we continue to examine factors in the environment, we will see how we can make a difference!

Not only are we influenced to buy certain foods (especially fast food, and we know how fat laden that is!), we are also influenced to try new diets, new diet aids, use exercise videos, or join a health club. Many of these can be sound weight management techniques, but be aware of any that promise "miracle" weight loss. IF IT SOUNDS TO GOOD TO BE TRUE, IT PROBABLY IS TOO GOOD TO BE TRUE! Refer to the Factor Twelve–Risk to explore these areas in greater detail.

You can have it all, you just can't have it all at once.

Oprah Winfrey

Not only does what we see and hear influence us, but the people who surround us every day have a great impact on our weight management program. Our families (addressed in Factor Five–Family), friends, and co-workers exert tremendous influence regarding this area. Ask yourself these questions:

- *Are my friends and co-workers supportive?*

- *Do my friends and co-workers have regular exercise habits?*

- *Do my extra-curricular activities with my friends always include food?*

- *Do my co-workers bring in doughnuts and other snacks to share?*

- *Do I have a refrigerator and/or microwave available at work so I can bring healthy lunches to eat?*

- *Am I respected the way I am?*

- *Do I feel pressured to conform to bad eating habits just because everyone does? (Just say no!)*

The work environment can be very detrimental to good weight management, but realize that people can be as much of a help as a hindrance. Don't be afraid to ask for help. Only you can make the real difference, but bringing others along can only multiply the gains!

Only from the alliance of everyone working with each other are great things born.

Anonymous

Now we are about to discuss some very serious concerns about the environment. According to the 1988 Surgeon General's report, "What we eat may affect our risk for several of the leading causes of death for Americans, notably, the degenerative diseases such as: atherosclerosis, coronary heart disease, strokes, diabetes, and some types of cancers. These disorders, together, now account for more than two-thirds of all deaths in the United States." That is really scary! So what does the environment have to do with this?

The answer is the increased use of processed food and contamination of the earth's food supply by "safe" chemicals and drugs given to animals raised for food consumption which have long-term effects that are not completely known or understood. So, now that you are afraid to eat any food at all, it should be easy to manage your weight! Really, this is not meant to be a scare tactic. It is important to be aware that many of the foods we eat are potentially harmful. What can we do? The answer is really simple! Avoid processed and fast foods and eat a balanced diet consisting of more vegetables, fruits, and whole grains than any other food. In fact, if you follow the American Dietary Association's guidelines discussed in Factor Seven–Education, you will have such a diet! (Remember that when we are using the word "diet" here, we are using it to describe your overall food choices, not a temporary device to lose weight.)

In addition to eating a well-balanced diet, exercise needs to be included as an integral part of your weight management program.

---

*In the power to change yourself is the power
to change the world around you.*
                                    Anwar Sadat

Once we become aware of the things that affect our eating and exercise choices, we can move to the acceptance of our responsibilities to search out our best options and make the best decisions. Good weight management is a process over time. If you have gained weight or are otherwise unhappy with your health or fitness level, chances are it did not happen overnight; reversing this process will take time. Don't be discouraged! You can do it!

An unknown travel agent told this story:

> *A woman who had booked a trip to Fresno, called and asked, "Do airlines put your physical description on your bag so they know whose luggage belongs to whom?"*

I said, "No, why do you ask?"

She replied, "Well, when I checked in with the airline, they put a tag on my luggage that said FAT, and I'm overweight, is there a connection?"

After putting her on hold for a minute while I "looked into it" I came back and explained that the city code for Fresno is FAT, and that the airline was just putting a destination tag on her luggage!

The law of culture is to let each of us become
all that we are capable of being.
Anonymous

✎ Activity

Refer to your journal activity previously completed in this chapter. Ask yourself these questions.

- What message influenced me to think about eating certain food?

- What was appealing about the message?

- Was I influenced to exercise?

- Do I find I want to eat because everyone else is eating?

- What physical image do I have for myself, and is it realistic?

Environment is the complex of social and cultural condi-tions affecting the nature of an individual or community.
American Heritage Dictionary

Factor

Environment

Wealth

We cannot bring prosperity by discouraging thrift.
We cannot help small men by tearing down big men.
We cannot help the poor by destroying the rich.
We cannot lift the wage earner by pulling down the wage payer.
We—governments or people—cannot keep out of trouble by spending more than we have.
We cannot further the brotherhood of man by inciting class hatred.
We cannot build character and courage by taking away initiative and independence.
We cannot help people permanently by doing for them what they could and should do for themselves.

We sometimes become so inundated by the fog of messages that surround us that we do not realize the influence the environment has on our lives. More and more Americans are finding themselves in a financial crisis! There are more credit card debt and bankruptcies than ever before. The Commerce Department put a microscope to our fiscal habits and found that incomes jumped 5.9 percent in 1999, but spending rose 7 percent. Savings dropped to an all-time annual low of 2.4 percent after taxes.

We ask ourselves why? The answer is clear and sometimes depressing. Everything with which we come in contact influences our thoughts and subliminally influences all of our decisions, including those regarding our financial well-being. It is necessary to be aware of these influences in order to control their effects on our decision-making process. (Okay, you're saying to yourself that you are not that easily influenced, but you are!)

Bargain; something you can't use
at a price you can't resist.

Franklin P. Jones

"The amount you see on the tag, ma'am," stated the salesman to the woman who was looking at a washing machine, "covers, city, state and federal taxes. The price is additional."

How easily are we influenced? Think about the last time you bought something just because that item was on sale. There are many times in a normal week when mixed/negative messages are telegraphed to our unsuspecting brains. We explored various influences in the weight factor that also apply to the wealth factor. These are listed again for your review. Think about the kinds of things that influence your spending habits.

- Billboards
- Advertising
- Television
- Radio

- Newspapers
- Magazines
- Floor displays in stores

✎ Activity

· ·

Use your journal and record all messages that you receive from the above categories (You may think of some of your own!) for one week. Write down the items that you were tempted to purchase because of the impression made by the things in your environment. Try to become aware of those things that influence you that you didn't know were influences... where are you most vulnerable?

Do we really need to spend our money on any of these items, or are we just being influenced by the message? Have you ever been shopping with a child who has been influenced by advertising they have seen? Maybe you were looking at paper towels and your child told you to buy Brand X because on TV it says that it is so strong it can hold a bowl even when it's wet! We realize that is just a claim, and we don't let it influence us, but are we always that aware?

Once we become aware of the things that affect our item choices, we can move to the acceptance of our responsibility to search out our best options and make the best decisions. You know that little voice that tells you whether you really do want to buy the item? Trust your instincts. If they tell you no, GOOD FOR YOU! Don't buy it.

Once we decide that we do want to make the purchase, we have to decide if we can actually afford the "bargain." Refer to your journal activity on budgeting and see how this purchase fits into your plan.

All television is educational television.
The question is, what is it teaching?
Nicholas Johnson

We have explored how the messages around us influence our spending. Now, let's take a look at how the people around us can influence what we buy (family will be addressed in Factor Five—Family). We sometimes limit our vision of what we feel is possible to the individuals in our immediate circle. Ask yourself these questions:

- *Are my friends and co-workers supportive?*

- *Do my friends and co-workers regularly go on shopping sprees?*

- *Do my extra-curricular activities with my friends often involve spending money?*

- *Do my co-workers dress in expensive, designer clothes?*

- *Do I feel the need to buy "trendy" clothes, or do I understand that "timeless" clothes are a better value?*

- *Do I feel inclined to go to the sale racks first or do I feel I have to pay full price for an item?*

- *Am I respected for whom I am not what I have?*

- *Do I feel pressured to conform to bad spending habits just because everyone does? (Remember it is quality, not quantity!)*

Is it important that a friend or associate has a bigger, better car; a more expensive home; designer clothes? Does that trigger any feelings of inadequacy, desire, need or jealousy? If we are motivated negatively by the fortunes of others, do we respond with a need to compete?

I can remember my mother asking me why I wanted an expensive record player. (I know I am showing my age.) I told her that all of my friends had a similar player. My mother replied, "If all of your friends jumped off a bridge, would you want to do that too?" There is nothing wrong with healthy competition, but make sure that competition does not cause financial stress to your budget!

There are a growing number of people who have overextended themselves financially. Count how many credit card applications you receive in a week. If you fall into the credit trap, you might find yourself joining the ever-increasing number of people who are one paycheck away from being homeless. Unfortunately, their only choice is filing bankruptcy, which accounts for the rising number of bankruptcies.

I know; that could never happen to you—right? I know you can make the right decisions. I believe in your ability to win the wealth battle.

---

*Tell me thy company, and I'll tell thee
what thou art.*

From Cervantes' Don Quixote

If you recognize the above scenario, you may find yourself
challenged by unnecessary decisions. Refer back to this
chapter when examining your goals and objectives, needs vs.
wants, and attitudes about wealth.

In our quest for answers, it is necessary to accept that we are
influenced by what we see, what we hear, what we say, and
with whom we associate. Not all relationships and messages in
the environment are negative. Our ability to distinguish
between what would be in our best interest or of consequence
will be a constant challenge in our struggle for success in
wealth management.

Buying is just one piece of the money management puzzle.
Once we have curtailed our unnecessary spending we have the
ability to plan for our secure financial future. Yes, I'm talking
about investments, and yes, you have the ability to increase
your wealth by the choices you make. Believe in yourself!
Investments play an important role and the investment
environment around us influences the choices we make.

---

*What you and I will become in the end
will be just more and more of what we
are deciding and trying to be right now.*

John Powell, S. J.

The good news is there is potential for your money to make money. The bad news is that there are a lot of factors that will encourage you to make the wrong decision. Remember: IF IT SOUNDS TOO GOOD TO BE TRUE, IT PROBABLY IS! Don't fall for those get-rich-quick schemes. Follow the suggestions in the recipe boxes that best suit your needs.

The folly of human nature is neatly summed up by the case of the middle-aged schoolteacher who invested her life savings in a business enterprise which had been elaborately explained to her by a swindler.

When her investment disappeared and the wonderful dream was shattered, she went to the office of the Better Business Bureau. "Why on earth," they asked, "didn't you come to us first? Didn't you know about the Better Business Bureau?"

"Oh yes," said the woman sadly. "I've always known about you. But I didn't come because I was afraid you'd tell me not to do it."

✎ Activity

●●

Refer to your journal activity previously completed in this chapter.
Ask yourself these questions.

- What message influenced me to think about making
  a purchase?

- What was appealing about the message?

- Was "keeping up with the Joneses" my motivation for
  thinking about making the purchase?

- Do I find I want to do more impulse buying than
  purchasing needed items?

Factor 2

Motivation

If you cannot accomplish one thing, move on to another which you can accomplish.
Al Kali

Factor

Motivation

Weight

Beauty Tips by Audrey Hepburn

For attractive lips, speak words of kindness.
For lovely eyes, seek out the good in people.
For a slim figure, share your food with the hungry.
For beautiful hair, let a child run his fingers through
it once a day.
For poise, walk with the knowledge you'll never walk alone.
People, even more than things, have to be restored, renewed,
revived, reclaimed and redeemed. Never throw out anybody.

Remember: if you ever need a helping hand, you'll find one at
the end of your arm. As you grow older you will discover that
you have two hands. One for helping yourself, the other for
helping others.

What motivating force will be the key to your weight management success? Once you are able to answer that question, you will be on your way to achieving that success.

Different things motivate us. Once we have an understanding of the motivating factors for weight management, we will have a better understanding of how to achieve success in weight management and maintain that success for the long term. The motivating factors are the starting point for a good weight management program. As odd as it may sound, sometimes weight management does not just mean weight loss. Weight management consists of controlling factors that affect our weight in ways that are unhealthy for us. The ultimate goal is a weight management program that keeps us happy and healthy.

The greatest happiness is to transform your feelings into actions.

Madame de Stael

Good Health–It seems everyone wants to be in good health. Is good health a motivating factor for you? Do you feel that good health will affect the rest of your life? With good health, we have more energy and a feeling of security to enable us to meet life's challenges.

Looking Good–Is looking good a factor that motivates you? What is your definition of looking good? Be sure to be realistic in your image of yourself. Know that your genetics will play a part in the way you look. You should strive to look the best you can for your body type, lifestyle, etc.

Self-esteem—Is self-esteem what motivates you? Do you believe that if you control your weight you will have more respect for yourself and from others? Do you feel that controlling your weight will help you be viewed as more successful? Most people are too hard on themselves when it comes to weight management. The important thing is to find the weight that is right for you and work toward that weight. When you have the skills to achieve this weight, you will feel better about yourself. When you feel better about yourself, others will feel better about you. As Carole King sang, "You've got to get up every morning with a smile on your face and show the world all the love in your heart! Then people gonna treat you better, you're gonna find, yes, you will, that you're beautiful as you feel."

Energy—Are you motivated by a need to have more energy in your daily life? If you have more energy, you will be motivated to work harder at your job and to enjoy your leisure time pursuits. You will find that life is more fulfilling and a lot more fun!

Satisfaction—Is satisfaction what motivates you? The ultimate feeling of gratification; you have reached your goals and achieved control of your weight. You are contented with your weight and have a feeling of well being. Your personal efforts helped you achieve your weight management success.

Competition—Is competition one of your motivators? Are you always trying to look like the model in the magazine, or the muscular guy at your gym? Everyone cannot look like Arnold Schwarzenegger, nor does everyone necessarily want to look like him! Are you jealous of others who appear to be in better shape than you are? Are you willing to use the strategies that will enable you to achieve the visual image you have of yourself?

Special Events–Is there a special event in the future that motivates you? Is it your class reunion, a wedding, a vacation? Do you want to slim down and/or gain muscle to look your best? When a special event is the motivator, decide in advance the time frame you have to achieve the look you desire. Only you can make it happen.

Favorite Outfit–Is wearing a favorite outfit a motivator for you? Perhaps you have a pair of pants that you really like, but the waist is too tight. Can you work out and control your eating to fit into the pants again? The satisfaction of wearing that favorite clothing item is a real confidence builder!

Fear of Failure–Is fear of failure what motivates you? Are you afraid that if you attempt weight management and fail, you will disappoint yourself and those around you? Are you afraid that you will not be able to do the things you want in your life if you don't have good weight management? Gaining control and good weight management are the stepping stones to a healthier you.

---

*Never measure the height of the mountain
until you have reached the top.*
                                    Dag Hammerskjold

What are some motivational obstacles you might encounter?

Age–Many people find that as they age, it is harder to lose weight than when they were younger. This could inhibit your motivation and make it easier for you to give up. Remember that as you age, certain types of fat become enzyme resistant to loss, and your metabolism often slows down. It is important to stick to your weight management plan to achieve results.

Time–Finding time to exercise can be difficult when juggling work and family. It is important to schedule time to exercise and to schedule time for meals. Eating on the run is detrimental to good weight management. Scheduling assists you in finding the time to eat sensibly and exercise. You also need to give yourself enough time to see the results of your weight management program.

Money–Joining a health club or joining a weight management program can be expensive. However, spending money is not a prerequisite for managing your weight. You can do everything you need to do in your own home or neighborhood. Walking is one of the best forms of weight management. Don't let money keep you from meeting your goals.

Family–Sometimes engaging in a weight management program collides with the demands of family. Is your family supportive? Does your culture help or inhibit establishing a good weight management plan? Perhaps the varied schedules of family members make one mealtime impossible. Try to start new habits and traditions that will assist you and your family develop a healthy, workable, weight management program.

Work Environment–Try to bring your lunch instead of going out to lunch. Avoid the doughnuts the boss brought to work in the morning. When there is a potluck on the job, bring food that you can eat sensibly. Share your knowledge with your co-workers.

Lack of Education–Remember to plan your eating and exercise. Have realistic expectations, goals and objectives, and realize that weight management is a long-term process. Don't be fooled by quick weight loss programs that make unrealistic promises. Sensible weight management will make a difference for the rest of your life.

Attitude–Don't put off until tomorrow that which you can do today. Start your weight management program today. If you decide to start, then put it off, too many things can happen to interfere with actually starting. Tell yourself you have the self-discipline, willpower, and determination to start today.

I am only an average man, but I work harder at it than the average man.
                                    Theodore Roosevelt

Finding out what triggers your motivation and captures your excitement will propel you into action.

✎ Activity

• Determine what motivates you.

• Establish your objectives based on that motivation.

• List the steps you need to take to achieve successful weight management.

• Use your journal to stay on track.

Seek not outside yourself, success is within.
Mary Lou Cook

Factor

Motivation

Wealth

The year was 1958. The Green Bay Packers ended their season with one win and ten losses. In 1959, new life was injected into this struggling football team. Vince Lombardi was the new coach and in the next nine years, led the Packers to a 75 percent winning record. The Packers accumulated five NFL championships, including winning the nation's first two Super Bowls.

How did they do it? Frank Gifford explained it this way: "It wasn't his knowledge of football strategy and tactics. No, it was his ability to motivate each player. Lombardi could get that extra 10 percent effort out of an individual." Gifford went on to explain the compounding effect: "Multiply 10 percent times forty men on the team times fourteen games in a season—and you're fast building a winning team. "

What motivating force will be the key to your financial success? Once you are able to answer that question, you will be on your way to achieving that success.

Different things motivate us. Once we understand what those things are, we will have a better understanding of how we achieve financial success and what money means to us.

Action, to be effective, must be directed to clearly conceived ends.

J. Nehru

Happiness—Is happiness what motivates you? Do you feel that if you had more money you would be able to stop living from paycheck to paycheck? You could relax and enjoy life. You would have a feeling of contentment with your financial condition.

Independence—Is independence what motivates you? With enough money you could buy financial freedom. You would have choices: work or not work, buy or not buy, and where and when to go on vacation. Your financial success would give you the freedom to do what you want.

Control—Is control what motivates you? With money you would be in control of your life; you would be a winner, not a loser. You would be strong enough to have total command over your life. You would be recognized as someone of importance. You would be personally accountable and involved in the management of your investment strategies.

Esteem–Is self-esteem what motivates you? You would have pride in yourself and your accomplishments, and others would recognize you as being successful and having worthiness. You worked hard and made the money to earn respect. You are motivated by the distinction and status your money would bring you.

Affection–Is affection what motivates you? If you had the money, do you feel you would be loved? Money makes life so much easier. You wouldn't be fighting with your loved ones over money. Your money decisions would not be guided by your feelings; you would show sensible and sound uses of your money.

Security–Is security what motivates you? If you had enough money you would be safe; you would feel no harm could come to you; money would protect you from all evil. When you evaluate your financial status, you would have peace of mind.

Satisfaction–Is satisfaction what motivates you? The great feeling of contentment that you have reached your financial goals and objectives? You would be pleased with where you were financially. You would have a feeling of well-being. Your personal efforts helped you achieve financial success.

Competition–Is competition what motivates you? Are you always trying to "keep up with the Joneses?" Are you jealous of others that have a more secure, profitable or solid financial future? Are you willing to implement the strategies that will put you a step above your perceived competition?

Fear–Is fear what motivates you? Are you afraid you will not have the money to do the things you've dreamed of doing? Things like graduating from college, buying that new home, providing for your family, sending your children to college, or having a secure financial future?

You do not have to be a genius to get rich, you just have to identify what motivates you to become rich and get to it.

If you can't change the circumstances, change your perspective.

What are some of the motivational enemies you might face?

Tedium–Finding your motivation from the excitement of the long-term goal rather than from the excitement of the moment will result in achieving success instead of the disappointment we feel when we recall our short-term failures.

Anxiety–You decide what motivates you, then you decide what to do to succeed, and you become uncomfortable. You begin to take the steps for success, but you begin to doubt your ability to live up to your potential. Just tell yourself "So I'm uncomfortable; live with it. It is irrelevant, knowing you will thrive!"

Risk–Are you making the right decisions for success? Have you allocated your portfolio properly, and are you willing to accept the risk that accompanies the higher return you can receive over time?

Have patience with all things, but chiefly,
have patience with yourself.
                                                St. Francis DeSales

---

Finding out what triggers your motivation and captures your excitement will propel you into action.

✎ Activity

· ·

- Determine what motivates you.
- Establish your objectives based on that motivation.
- List the steps you need to take to achieve financial success.
- Use your journal to stay on track.

Seek not outside yourself, success is within.
                        Unknown

Factor 3

Attitude

> *It is time for us all to cheer for the doer, the achiever—the one who recognizes the challenge and does something about it.*
>
> Vince Lombardi

Factor

Attitude

Weight

John got up, looked in the mirror and exclaimed, "I feel so fat today. Nothing fits me anymore and I don't even know why I should try. Maybe I should just go out and buy a new suit...one that fits! Then I can eat all I want!" Across the street, Ray looked in the mirror and said, "I really need to gain control of my body. My eating and exercise habits have been horrible. Today I will start a new way of life and return to my former fitness level."

Studies show that the way you think and feel about your weight and size play a key role in your attitude and how successful you will be in a weight management program.

Becoming overweight and out of shape may be the outcome of behavior you have with food and your attitude toward exercise. Your use of food may, for instance, indicate manipulating or taking control of at least one aspect of your life. It can also be a result of a hectic lifestyle. You may have good intentions about exercising, but you just do not have the time! You have to decide that exercise is as important to your life as eating and drinking, and that you need to make the time for exercise! You have to do it for your health and longevity. You can change your attitude and make it posi- tive.

If we feel that we have no control in other areas of our life, we may decide that what we eat will be our decision, even though it may be a bad decision.

The bottom line is that substan- tial aspects of inner reality and self-image exert powerful influences on the body process. (That is not to say that weight management prob- lems lay only in the mind. Many people have physical and medical concerns that affect their ability to manage weight. Always consult with your doctor to determine any underlying causes of weight management problems.) No matter the cause, your attitude will influence your ability to control and manage your weight. In addition, you will find that as you exercise more, your energy level may increase and you will feel better about yourself. As your physical body changes, so does your internal image of yourself. Exercise/

attitude is one of those vicious cycles, but it is a good vicious cycle because the more you exercise, the better your attitude, and the better your attitude, the more you want to exercise!

Nurture the dreams that inspire you to go beyond your limits.

Author Unknown

Look for the real cause of your weight management problems in your mind and body. You need to be an observer and evaluate your specific signals and analyze the personal behavior that might affect your weight, health, and fitness level.

- *Create a mental picture of yourself as a healthy and fit person. Is that picture realistic?*

- *When you speak to yourself or have inner dialogue, be objective about what your hear. You then will be able to find out what attitudes, assumptions and beliefs are most frequently behind your actions and behavior.*

- *Consult with your doctor to determine any medical or other causes of your weight management problems.*

- *Find time to exercise: write it down and schedule it if need be.*

- *Establish a pattern of exercise that works for you.*

- *Write down in your journal your commands, criticism, encouragement, and everything that makes up your inner dialogue. Keep track of time spent exercising. Go back every day and read what you have written. Make an effort to change the negatives of the day before into positives today.*

The real act of discovery consists not in
finding new lands, but in seeing with new eyes.
Marcel Proust

Ask yourself, "What is it I want to accomplish?"

Tune into your inner self and evaluate your wants.

Take control of your life.

Involve those around you in your goals and objectives.

Thank those who have helped you in your journey.

Understand that patience is vital for success.

Dreams are not goals until you act on them.

Expect the best of yourself and you will be rewarded.

These are discoveries that will assist you in making the attitude adjustment needed to become a healthy and fit person.

The main thing is to be patient with yourself, give yourself the gift of time, and just as important, the permission to make mistakes. Expect problems, so that when they come you will be prepared to handle them.

Ask yourself these questions:

- *How do I determine what I will eat?*

- *Does the fact that I know I am eating something "bad" for me keep me from eating it?*

- *Do I feel in control when I am eating?*

- *Once I make a bad decision, am I willing to stop there and eat well the rest of the day?*

- *Do I exercise regularly?*

- *How important is exercise to my lifestyle?*

- *If I miss an exercise workout, do I give up, or go back the next day?*

There is something that is much rarer than
ability: the ability to recognize ability.
Robert Hall

Most of our food habits have an emotional dimension. They can make you feel bad, good or satisfied. We need to understand that trying to stuff down our emotions with food will not work. It is a game you can not win. We can use exercise as a tool to change those emotions. Studies have shown that people who exercise regularly have a better self-image than those who do not. Exercise benefits the mind and body.

Spring is when you feel like whistling even
with a shoe full of slush.
Doug Larson

We are always going to have emotions or attitudes both negative and positive. If you make a dash for the refrigerator every time you start to feel a negative, you will pay the price in weight gain very quickly. Instead of dashing for the refrigerator, do ten push-ups or ten sit-ups.

Successful attitude management depends on:

- *Looking at yourself honestly; changing what you can and accepting what you cannot*

- *Being responsive to your self: your moods, stress, etc.*

- *Being aware of others' interaction with your eating habits*

- *Disconnecting food from emotions*

- *Not using your current fitness level to control your eating and exercise habits*

- *Realizing that only you can control your attitude*

Try to disconnect food from your emotions, and if you are successful you will have accomplished two things:

- *Your weight will no longer be dependent on your feelings.*

- *When you release your emotions and allow yourself to experience them, you will give yourself permission to deal with them.*

✎ Activity

• •

Here are some questions to answer. Think about how these relate to your weight attitude. Use your journal to record all responses.

- Do I usually have a positive attitude?
  ○ Yes   ○ No

- Am I usually flexible when dealing with issues?
  ○ Yes   ○ No

- Do I usually live in the present, seeing a clear and optimistic view of the future?
  ○ Yes ○ No

- Do I usually live in the past, spending too much time in what could have been?
  ○ Yes ○ No

Ask yourself these questions:

1. Why am I eating?

2. Do I regularly eat when I am not hungry?

3. Am I using food for comfort?

4. Do I regularly eat on impulse?

5. Am I happy with my weight and fitness level?

6. How do I visualize myself?

7. When I was eating was I:
   Anxious?
   Angry?
   Bored?
   Afraid?
   Depressed?

> The quality of a person's life is in direct proportion to their commitment to excellence.
> *Bishop Gore*

Factor

Attitude

Wealth

Money is not the kernel. We all know that money is a relative matter. Do you recall what Ibsen said about money? "Money may be the husk of many things, but not the kernel. It brings you food, but not appetite; medicine, but not health; acquaintances, but not friends; servants, but not loyalty; days of joy, but not peace or happiness."
 - Lionel Crocker, Professor of Speech, Denison University

What does your money mean to you? The answer to that question will have a lot to do with how you spend, save and use your money.

Does your money control you, or do you control your money? Begin by analyzing and understanding your attitudes whether they are right or wrong, bad or good. Determine how adequate you feel when making money decisions. What money choices have you made in the past, and what motivated your decision?

Take a realistic look at your own general attitudes about money. The hardest thing we can do is really look at ourselves. I know, sometimes we do not like what we see, but come on, take a look.

To be successful in managing your money, you must:

- *Have self-perception. Are you willing to look at yourself honestly; accept what you can't change and change what you can?*

- *Be responsive and conscious of the people around you. We usually have to make money decisions with others, or that will affect others, so take into account that our money attitudes will affect others.*

- *Be willing to educate yourself so that your understanding of how money works will make the flow of your money affairs and transactions go smoothly.*

It is important to know that our attitude about money is one thing we can control. Once we evaluate our behavior, and see a positive pattern, we can build on it. However, if we see a negative pattern, we can take the steps needed to turn that negative into a positive. Okay, admit it, you do have negative thoughts sometimes, right?

Ask yourself these specific questions about spending and saving to determine positive and negative patterns of your own.

- *How do I determine if I will make a big purchase?*

- *Does the fact that I will have to charge the item deter me from making the purchase?*

- *Am I willing to wait, save the money, and then buy the item?*

- *Once I make the decision, am I willing to move on, or do I moll over my decision?*

- *Do I feel in control when I make money decisions?*

As a man thinks, so he is.

Proverbs 23:7

"Some young people complain as if the world owed them a living. Nobody owes anybody anything; it's up to each individual to set high standards for himself or herself, and to set about working hard and creating a solid future. I see more energy, life, and spirit in many so-called senior citizens than in numerous young people I've come in contact with."

- Katharine Hepburn

Remember you *can* teach an old dog new tricks! So take control, change how you think and your bad habits, and watch your financial gain.

Wisdom is knowing what to do.
Skill is knowing how to do it.

Thomas Jefferson

Don't confuse attitude with feelings. We sometimes feel a certain way: mad, depressed, afraid or sad, but we still hold on to a positive mental attitude.

Let us assume you have car trouble: you are angry because you have to spend money to have it fixed. A positive mental attitude will help you sort through your options. To successfully pay for the large expense do you:

- *Put the expense on a charge card because it is easy, you are angry, and you just want to get it paid?*

- *Empty your savings, leaving you with no financial cushion?*

- *Finance the repairs with a bank?*

- *Borrow the money from family or friends?*

- *Buy a new car?*

It is that positive attitude that allows us to have hope. Those of us that maintain a positive attitude tend to be more open and flexible.

ATTITUDE
By Charles Swindoll

"The longer I live the more I realize the impact of attitude on life. Attitude, to me, is more important than facts. It is more important than the past, than education, than money, than circumstances, than failures, than successes, than what other people think or say or do. It is more important than appearance, giftedness, or skill. It will make or break a company...a church...a home. The remarkable thing is we have a choice every day regarding the attitude we will embrace for that day. We cannot change our past...we cannot change the fact that people will act in a certain way. We cannot change the inevitable. The only thing we can do is play on the one string we have, and that is our attitude...I am convinced that life is 10 percent what happens to me and 90 percent how I react to it. And so it is with you...we are in charge of our Attitudes."

✎ Activity

Record your patterns and attitudes for saving and spending.

These are some of the same questions asked in the weight section. Think about where you would rate yourself as far as your attitude toward wealth. Answer these questions in your journal, and then come back to these answers after you've had the time to work on your attitude if needed.

- Do I usually have a positive attitude?
  ○ Yes ○ No

- Am I usually flexible when dealing with issues?
  ○ Yes ○ No

- Do I usually live in the present, seeing a clear and optimistic view of the future?
  ○ Yes ○ No

- Do I usually live in the past, spending too much time in what could have been?
  ○ Yes ○ No

Ask yourself these questions:

1. Why am I spending?

2. Do I regularly spend when I don't need anything?

3. Am I using money for comfort?

4. Do I regularly spend on impulse?

5. Am I happy with my savings?

6. Can I see myself wealthy?

7. When I spent money was I:
   Anxious?
   Angry?
   Bored?
   Afraid?
   Depressed?

Factor 4

Habits

> We are what we repeatedly do.
> Excellence, then is not an act, but
> a habit.
>
> *Aristotle*

Factor 4

Habits

Weight

Did you know that in the 1500s people cooked in the kitchen in a big kettle that always hung over the fire? Every day they lit the fire and added things to the pot. They mostly ate vegetables and didn't get much meat. They would eat the stew for dinner, leaving leftovers in the pot to get cold overnight and then start over the next day. Sometimes the stew had food in it that had been in there for a month. Hence the rhyme: "peas porridge hot, peas porridge cold, peas porridge in the pot nine days old."

Your habits will influence how you structure your eating schedule, what you will eat, and how much you will exercise. Habit-observation exercises are an integral part of your personal weight loss program. Before you can begin changing your eating and exercise habits, you must first identify them clearly. Use your journal and do this in writing. If you write it down, you will not forget it. By writing down your observations of your eating and exercise patterns, you will increase your awareness of your destructive habits, which are your "secret" attitudes and feelings about what you eat and how you exercise.

If you have been keeping a journal of what you eat and how much you exercise, you will continue keeping a journal, but this time with a slightly different purpose. The purpose of this journal activity is to observe your eating habits and the influences that trigger them into action. You will also examine whether or not you exercise, and if not, why you do not.

Begin these exercises now. Take time to do them calmly, deliberately, and with patience. Do not expect to complete them in one sitting. You did not develop your eating and exercise habits in one day. You will not become consciously aware of all of them in one day either. Work on these exercises throughout your program, preferably during a quiet time you set aside for yourself each day.

When keeping this journal, write down how you felt before and after your decision to eat a particular food. Identifying what triggered you to eat a certain food might help you decide whether or not it was a good food choice. Identify when you exercise, and what motivates you to continue/begin exercising.

What you value is what you think about.
What you think about is what you become.
                                    Joel Weldon

Once you have begun to recognize your eating and exercise habits, you can begin to look closely at the habits you have developed in selecting your food and workout choices. It is likely that you have these habits with very little conscious awareness, because you probably learned some of them from your parents. To start to identify these eating and exercise habits, you must begin by questioning them.

In completing this exercise, answer these questions by writing out the actual habit you practice. Add questions that pertain to your own lifestyle.

1. Do you eat everything on your plate without thinking about the portion sizes? Are you eating because you are hungry? Is it a habit because as a child you always had to clean your plate?

2. How fast do you eat your food? Do you chew slowly? Do you put your fork down between bites?

3. Do you use food as a comfort? Do you think about food all day long?

4. How often do you eat?

5. Do you plan a menu for the day and stick to it? Do you make a shopping list for the grocery store and stick to it? Do you avoid impulse buying?

6. Do you think about all the food you want to eat whether you are hungry or not?

7. When you eat for emotional comfort, what do you tend to eat and why?

8. Can you eat moderately?

9. Do you ask yourself "Do I really need to eat this?"

10. How often do you exercise?

11. Do you make excuses for not exercising?

12. Do you find activities you enjoy to include in your exercises?

13. Are you "afraid" to exercise for fear of what others may think?

14. Do you make a plan for exercise?

Chains of habit are too light to be felt until they are too heavy to be broken.
                                    Warren Buffet

Weight: To Do Habits:

- *Acknowledge the reality of your eating, the desire to eat, and the eating habits supporting the desire.*

- *Express the willingness to confront your "secret" desire to eat and acknowledge responsibility for that desire and its effect on your overall weight goal.*

- *Allow yourself to honestly feel the genuine desire to change, do not just wishfully think about it.*

- *Be honest enough with yourself to admit that not changing is a far more painful and difficult way to live than actively choosing to live your life as a healthy, secure person.*

- *Actively use your self-honesty as a form of internal strength with which to make the choice to live a healthy lifestyle and be willing to do what is necessary and keep doing the right thing for the rest of your life.*

✎ Activity

Once you are committed to change your bad habits you need to:

- Watch yourself. Observe and discover the principal characteristics of your eating and exercise habits.

- Watch other people. Observe and discover characteristics of others you respect that have good eating habits.

- Create a supportive environment. Get family and professional support; decide whether to include the people around you in your eating plan.

- Recognize that bad habits are not forever. It's hard to teach an old dog new tricks, but not impossible.

Say these affirmations:

- – I am responsible for what I eat.

- – It is okay to make myself happy.

- – It is okay to enjoy my food.

- – Eating will not make me happy, but I need to eat properly for good health.

– I enjoy making good food choices.

– The more I make good food choices, the better I feel.

– I am a very special person.

– I expect others to accept me.

– I am able to change my bad eating habits to good eating habits.

– I pursue my goals.

– I deserve success.

– I want to have a healthy weight loss plan.

– I deserve to have a healthier lifestyle.

Write your own affirmations:

_____

_____

_____

_____

_____

_____

> *To change one's life start immediately.*
> *Do it flamboyantly. No exceptions!*
> *William James*

Factor

Habits

Wealth

If I had my life to live over, I'd dare to make more mistakes next time. I'd relax, I'd limber up. I would be sillier than I've been this trip. I would take fewer things seriously, take more chances, take more trips. I'd climb more mountains, and swim more rivers. I would eat more ice cream and less beans. I would, perhaps, have more actual troubles, but I'd have fewer imaginary ones.....
  —Anonymous

Your lifestyle and, most importantly, your habits will influence how you structure your financial well being.

As with the weight "habit" factor, habit-observation exercises are an integral part of your personal financial program. Before you can begin to change your financial habits, you must first *identify them clearly*. The best way to do this is on paper. If you write them down, you will not forget them. Remember that memory failure is a poor financial tactic, and will keep you from being financially secure. By writing down your observations of your spending patterns, you will increase your awareness of destructive habits, which are your "secret" attitudes and feelings about money.

For those of you who have kept behavior journals while following your financial plan, you will see that you will be doing things differently this time. The purpose of keeping a journal is to observe your money habits and the influences that trigger them into action.

Begin these exercises now, as you did for the weight "habit" factor. Take time to do them calmly, deliberately, and with patience. Do not expect to complete them in one sitting. Just like your weight habits, you did not develop your money habits in one day; you will not become consciously aware of all of them in one day either. Work on these exercises throughout your program, preferably during a quiet time you set aside for yourself each day.

I do not recommend writing down your observations immediately after spending or making a money decision. If you try to watch your desire to spend or make bad money choices too closely, you might decide that changing would be too overwhelming.

Once you have begun to recognize your money habits, you can begin to look closely at the habits you've developed in selecting your money choices. It is likely that you are only semi-consciously aware of these habits because you probably learned some of them from your parents. (See Factor Five–Family) To begin to identify these money habits, you must begin by questioning them.

In completing this exercise, do not answer just yes or no to the following questions. Write out the actual habit you practice. Add questions that pertain to your own lifestyle.

1. How fast do you spend your money? If you put extra money in your wallet, do you buy something whether you need it or not?

2. How much extra money do you feel you need to keep in your wallet to feel comfortable?

3. Do you rob Peter to pay Paul? And if Peter doesn't get paid, do you charge it?

4. How often do you shop?

5. Do you make a shopping list and stick to it?

6. Do you think about all the "stuff" you want to buy whether you need it or not?

7. When you spend for emotional comfort, what do you tend to buy?

8. What do you tell yourself when you spend? Do you say you're buying for others, when you are really buying for your self? (Something you want, but don't need?)

9. Can you spend moderately?

10. Do you think about what you spend?

11. Do you ask yourself "Do I really need to buy this?"

Wealth: To-Do Habits:

- *Acknowledge the reality of your spending, the desire to spend, and the spending habits supporting the desire.*

- *Express the willingness to confront your "secret" desire to spend, and acknowledge responsibility for that desire and its effect on your savings.*

- *Allow yourself to honestly feel the genuine desire to change; do not just wishfully think about it.*

- *Be honest enough with yourself to admit that not changing is a far more painful and difficult way to live than actively choosing to live your life as a financially secure person with choices you otherwise would not have.*

- *Actively use your self-honesty as a form of internal strength with which to make the choice to live financially secure. Be willing to do what is necessary, and keep doing the right thing for the rest of your life.*

✎ Activity

....

Once you're committed to change your bad habits you need to:

- Watch yourself. Observe and discover the principal characteristics of your spending habits.

- Watch other people. Observe and discover characteristics of others you respect that have good money habits.

- Create a supportive environment. Get family and professional support; decide whether to include the people around you in your saving plan.

- Recognize that bad habits are not forever. It's hard to teach an old dog new tricks, but not impossible.

Say these affirmations:
- I'm responsible for how I spend my money.

- It's okay to make myself happy.

- It's okay to have money.

- It's okay to save money.

- Money will not make me happy, only comfortable.

- I enjoy saving money.

- The more I save, the more I like it.

- I am a very special person.

- I expect others to accept me.

- I am able to change my bad money habits to good money habits.

- I pursue my goals.

- I deserve success.

- I like to be financially secure.

- I deserve to have a healthy financial future.

Write your own affirmations:

_____

_____

_____

_____

_____

_____

Factor 5

Family

> *The most important work you and I will ever do will be within the walls of our own homes.*
>
> *Harold B. Lee*

Factor

Family

Weight

Wise Advice from Kids:
- *Never trust a dog to watch your food.*
- *Never tell your mom her diet's not working.*
- *Stay away from prunes.*
- *You can't hide a piece of broccoli in a glass of milk.*
- *When your dad is mad and asks you, "Do I look stupid?" don't answer him.*

Family has a significant impact on everything we do, and successful weight management is no different. Our childhood experiences and genetics, coupled with our current lifestyle, connect the way we currently deal with weight management. Was your family fat or thin? Where does your family "carry" excess fat mass? What were your family eating patterns? How did your parents deal with weight management?

All of these issues of the past relate to the way we deal with these same issues today. If you had a regular mealtime as a child, that is probably something you strive for in your lifestyle today. Your memories of the foods you ate as a child, what type of family celebrations you had, how your family used food, etc. affect your attitudes today. The actions your parents took when they dealt with weight management are learned by you. We watched them and remembered...many events stay with us today.

We could have very unrealistic, confusing attitudes about the meaning and value of weight management, and what it might mean to us. As a child, a friend of mine can remember her mother weighing her potato chips so as not to over eat. Her mother, Mary, often counted calories as a way to control her weight, even though she was never really overweight (Maybe that is one of the reasons why ... she used successful strategies all her life to maintain control!). How she looked was important to her, and she took the necessary steps to achieve her goals. She realized that weight management was an ongoing process, one that she tried to maintain throughout her life.

Don't worry that your children never listen to you;
worry that they are always watching you.
Robert Fulghum

What kind of messages did you receive as a child?

Did your parents make you eat everything on your plate before you could eat dessert? Today we know that cleaning your plate should not be a prerequisite for dessert. In fact, many weight management programs advise you to always leave a small amount of food on your plate.

Did your parents use food as a reward? Did they tell you that if you were good you could get candy or ice cream? While that is not all bad, it inadvertently reinforces that food is a reward, rather than the idea of food being nutrition. Eat what you need, then stop!

Did your parents send mixed messages about food? Did they talk about controlling weight, yet insist you clean your plate, even if you were really full? Sometimes parents are worried that their children are not receiving the proper nutrition, and will make the child sit at the table until the food is gone. Many children tell stories of this nature. This belief has made some people overeat as adults.

Eat when you are hungry; drink when you are dry.
You just have to push yourself away from the table.
Joe Gardina

We may not realize it, but our parents' attitudes about weight management affect our attitudes. Just because your parents had certain attitudes, that does not mean that you have to be just like them. A major difference between 25-30 years ago and now is the emphasis on exercise and amount of fat consumed. How our parents were raised influenced them, and they were probably unaware of the legacy they were leaving us. We learned our eating habits from our families, which tend to be passed down from generation to generation. If these habits are positive, then we have a healthy outlook on weight management. What we need to do is sort out the good things we learned, and add the new revelations that will help us embark on a successful weight management program.

A good home must be made, not bought.
Joyce Maynard

Okay, how do you do that? Answer these questions:

1. Did you always eat everything on your plate? Did you feel satisfied or over full if forced to eat? Is this a habit to continue?

2. Did your family have a regular mealtime? Did you eat supper as a family? Will this work for you and is it valuable to you?

3. In what era did you grow up? Did you always have enough food to eat, or did you compete with siblings to have enough food? If food was sometimes scarce, does this make you eat more today? Is that a habit to continue? Did you grow up eating "fast food?" or eating "on the run?"

4. Did your parents use food as a reward, or did they stress the nutritional value of food? Do you eat for entertainment, gratification, etc., or because you are hungry?

5. Did your parents exercise? Many "baby boomers" did not learn good exercise habits from their parents because exercise was not stressed as part of good weight management at that time. Are you an exerciser?

6. Did your parents work outside the home? Did this encourage snacking until parents got home?

> *To know oneself is to study oneself in action*
> *with another person.*
> *Bruce Lee*

Now that you have evaluated your childhood weight management experiences, what's happening today?

Whatever stage of life you are living now has family implications.

> *One's first book, kiss, home run, is always the best.*
> *Clifton Fadiman*

If you are starting out on your own and living independently for the first time, you may be excited about your new adventure! Keep in mind that your weight management decisions (as with wealth decisions) will be based on your habits, needs, goals and dreams.

Your might be looking ahead toward:

- *Getting a new job—You may decide that you need to change your weight or your physical shape before interviewing. You will have to plan for the weight loss and change in fitness habits. Do you have enough time to achieve your goals?*

- *Going to your first class reunion—Does thinking about such an event trigger good or bad habits? Do you feel ready to meet your former classmates, or do you want to make a change?*

- *College life—You've heard about the freshmen ten. All that cafeteria food can pack on the weight. Are you ready to deal with the change in eating habits?*

- *First apartment—Now this is an adjustment. If living alone, can you plan nutritious meals for one, or will you eat out much of the time? If you have one or more than one roommate, will they be supportive or sabotage your efforts?*

- *Getting married—Most people want to look their best on such an important day. Are you satisfied with how you look, or do you want to make changes?*

In the absence of certainty,
instinct is all you can follow.
Jonathan Cainer

If you are married, without children, your weight management decisions might include:

- *Eating at home—Do you have a system to eat at home? Who will cook?*

- *Dining out frequently—Do you and your spouse ride to work together? Is it easier to eat on the way home rather than cook at home?*

- *Partying with friends—Will you go out after work for happy hour with friends?*

- *Regular mealtimes—Do you have a "three martini" lunch, or do you bring your lunch to work? Do you work through lunch or take a specified time for lunch? How about dinner? Do you arrive home at the same time each evening?*

- *Regular exercise—Do you stop at the gym on the way home and work out before dinner? Do you eat a nutritious snack before you work out to give you energy to sustain the workout?*

- *Evening snacking—Are you watching TV? Do you snack while watching? Do you go to the refrigerator during commercials? Are you aware of how much you are eating while watching TV?*

Real communication happens when people feel safe.
Ken Blanchard

If you are married with children, your goals will undoubtedly relate to your family and the interactions of the family.

You may need to think about:

- *Children's activities—Are you on the go...eating in the car?*

- *Regular meal times—With all the activities, is it possible to have one regular mealtime? Do you cook in shifts and as a result, eat each time you cook?*

- *Evening snacking—Now that you have some "quiet" time, do you eat for comfort?*

- *Teaching your children good habits—What are you teaching them? Is food a bribe or reward, or are you exemplifying good habits?*

- *Stress—Are you more concerned about having the time and money to devote to your family? How can you give everyone what is needed and still take care of yourself?*

---

*There's no cap on success. The jury stays
out till you take your last breath.*

Judy Sheindlin

If you are nearing retirement or are an empty nester, your goals
again change. Now your weight management decisions will be
based on adapting to the change in lifestyle, planning for
retirement, and being healthy for the rest of your life.

You may need to consider:

- *Smaller appetite—Are you eating meals that are nutritious and
  not too filling? Are you getting the most nutritious calories
  possible?*

- *Adjusting to cooking for one or two—Do you cook large portions
  and freeze some for a future meal? Do you dine out frequently?*

- *Increased leisure time—Are you exercising regularly
  now that you have more time? How are you spending
  your leisure time? Are you keeping your mind as well as
  your body active?*

It is important in any weight management program to involve
family, roommates, significant other, etc. Talk about the goals
and objectives. Find the common ground shared and see how
all can work to support each other. Include others in the meal
planning decisions. Try to supply food that is satisfying, yet
nutritious for all. Be a team... Together
                          Everyone
                          Achieves
                          More!

✎ Activity

....

Use your journal to answer the questions asked earlier in this factor. Determine the degree you want to be personally responsible and involved in the management of your weight.

Think about the following and jot down answers to these in your journal. How do your answers to both sets of questions correlate?

- Do you experience satisfaction at the way you handle your weight?

- Do you make emotional decisions when it comes to managing your weight?

- Do you find it more satisfying to use good eating habits, or do you eat for comfort?

- Do you have a high degree of anxiety when you think about managing your weight?

- Do you feel that if you work hard and do what you know is nutritionally sound, you will be happy with your weight management?

- Do you feel that if you have good weight management you will be happy?

- Do you feel that if you have good weight management you have power and control over your life?

- Do you feel in control of your weight management?

- Do you feel you are taking risks with your health and weight management?

- Do you dwell on past decisions you made concerning your weight management?

- Do you believe that you can establish good weight management techniques?

Whatever you are be a good one
Anonymous

Fctor

Family

Wealth

For 85 percent of American families, it is difficult to sit down and discuss money issues. Resentment can build until there is an explosion over something else, when the root of the problem is how money is spent in the household. What is surprising to me is that we don't connect our early childhood experiences with money to how we currently deal with our finances.

Our memory reveals struggles our parents might have had with the dollar. Perhaps we watched them delight, get discouraged, or argue over money. The actions our parents took when they dealt with their money just reinforced the fact that having or not having enough money has consequences. We watched the outcome, and how we remember those events stays with us.

We could have very unrealistic, confusing attitudes about the meaning and value of money and what money might mean to us.

Whether we realize it or not, what we remember about how our parents dealt with money, whether consciously or unconsciously, affects our money styles and habits. Our parents probably had no intentions of giving us negative feelings when it came to money, but when we received these messages, we were unaware that we needed to sort them out and understand the influences they had on us.

---

*Confidence is the inner voice that says you
are becoming what you are capable of being.*
Author Unknown

Depending on how your parents were raised, if they weren't taught the meaning or the limitations of money, neither were you.

If your parents lived during the Depression and had no money, you saw them saving for emergencies and being prudent. When spending money, they were only buying what was necessary. Perhaps your parents had plenty of money growing up and you saw that money represented prestige and status. These things would positively or negatively affect how you perceived your parents and their finances.

---

*Destiny is not a matter of chance, it is a
matter of choice.*
William Jennings Bryan

What mixed messages did you receive?

Your parents say, *"Money can't buy happiness."* However, you see them upset when they can't afford to buy that new car, or new house, etc.

Your parents tell you, *"Money isn't important,"* but you hear them arguing over the unpaid bills.

Your parents tell you, *"Save your money to buy those important items you've been wanting,"* but you see them charging groceries.

Your parents tell you, *"Money should not be your motivating factor for doing well,"* but you're rewarded with money when you bring home a good report card or you behave well at the doctor.

Most of the time we are not taught the meaning or the limitations that money has. We are not taught how to save, manage, or spend our money. We grow up, go out on our own, we open a bank account, apply for a credit card, and proceed to make terrible money mistakes and wonder why.

When we were young, did money always seem to be available (or maybe it wasn't available at all and was limited) to buy those school clothes and supplies, Christmas presents, vacations, etc.? What did we think?

- Money grows on trees.
- Go to the bank and get more.
- Write a check.

Since the supply of money may have seemed unlimited, we would get angry or confused when we were denied access.

Many of us are seriously affected by the way our parents handled money. We learn our money habits from our families, which tend to be passed down from generation to generation. If these habits are positive, we learn that money is a tool to be used for our maximum benefit, or if negative that it can cause many problems.

Okay, now what? Answer these questions:

1. Did you always get what you asked for, or were you often disappointed that your parents couldn't afford the things you asked for?

2. Did your parent give you an allowance, or did you just ask for money and receive it?

3. Did your friends have more money than you did, nicer cars, home, etc.? Were your parents wealthy, middle class or poor?

4. How much anger that involved money can you remember?

5. In what era did you grow up: Depression, Baby Boomer, Generation X or later?

6. Did you grow up with both parents in the home?

7. Did both of your parents work outside the home?

8. Were you rewarded with money; was money a controlling factor in your life? Is the person you are married to also controlling you with money?

9. Do you find yourself hesitant to use money for fun or pleasure? If you were able to spend your money on something wonderful, would you?

10. Were your parents afraid there would not be enough money? Is one of your fears today that you will never have enough money?

Now that we've evaluated our childhood money experiences, what is happening today?

Whatever stage of life you are living now has family implications.

If you are living independently, your money decisions will be based on your habits, needs, goals, and dreams. You might be looking ahead toward:
- *Continuing education*
- *First apartment*
- *First job*
- *First opportunity to save for retirement*
- *Partying with friends instead of saving money*

Wife to husband: "You keep saying money isn't worth much these days, but then you make a fuss when I spend some."

If you are married, without children, your money decisions might include:
- *Eating at home*
- *Dining out frequently*
- *Partying with friends*
- *Buying a new car*
- *Buying a new home*
- *Adjusting to different money habits (who pays for what?)*
- *Money kept separate or pooled together*

Perhaps you're married with children; your money decisions may be:
- *Eating at fast food restaurant or cooking at home*
- *Buying a bigger home*
- *Spending money on children's activities*
- *Saving for college*
- *Teaching your children good money habits*
- *Saving for retirement*
- *Helping out elderly parents*

If you become suddenly single, your money decisions may be:
- *Re-adjusting to a single income*
- *Buying a car*
- *Selling a home*
- *Buying a condominium*
- *Children's education*
- *Continuing your education*
- *Retirement income*

It is important in any wealth accumulation program to involve the people around you that will impact your decisions. Communication is the key to success...   Sharing the
Understanding and
Cooperation leads to
Communication for
Easy
Strategies to provide financial
Satisfaction

✎ Activity

Use your journal to answer the questions asked previously in this factor.

Determine the degree you want to be personally responsible and involved in the management of your money.

- Do you experience satisfaction at the way you handle your money?

- Do you make emotional decisions when it comes to money?

- Do you find it more satisfying to give than receive?

- Do you have a high degree of anxiety when you spend your money?

- Do you feel that if you work hard and do what you love the money will come?

- Do you feel that if you have enough money you will be happy?

- Do you feel that if you have money you have power?

- Do you feel in control of your finances?

- Are you comfortable with taking risks with your money?

- Do you dwell on past decisions you made with your money?

- Do you trust others with your money, or would you rather manage it yourself?

Factor 6

Budget

> *Plans are only good intentions unless they*
> *immediately degenerate into hard work.*
> *Peter B. Drucker*

Factor

Budget

Weight

How much you eat and the energy you expend are the keys to
the budgeting process of weight management. It is a simple
process of the choices you make. You are what you eat! You've
heard that time and time again. To help budget, you have to
decide if you are eating to satisfy your hunger (eating what is
necessary), or eating to satisfy your appetite (eating for enjoy-
ment). Eating, however, is only part of the equation. Your
activity level (yes, I'm talking about exercise) affects your
overall health and weight management, too!

Everything you eat and in how much activity you engage have
end results. If you know what you eat, when you eat, why you
eat, how much you eat, and how much you exercise, you can
begin to manage your weight. Aargh! Enough Charlie Brown!
Right now you may be feeling overwhelmed! Don't be! It is
really not that difficult to determine. Try this:

- *Use your journal to record <u>everything</u> you eat for the next week, and <u>all</u> the exercise you do.*

- *Decide which foods you think are good for you and which are not. Give the good foods a (+), the bad foods a (−). (Hopefully you have more +'s than −'s!)*

- *Organize your eating habits into times of day; record if you were hungry, how you were feeling, why you ate, and what you ate.*

- *Record all types and duration of all exercise—walking, gardening, cleaning, biking, etc.*

- *Create a mental picture of how you want to look.*

Now that you have looked at what you currently eat and how much activity you do, you have to take control.

Determine the times of day you eat, how much you eat, and if the amount you eat fluctuates based on certain situations. Decide the foods you eat that you know are not good for you, or foods that should be eaten in moderation. Many of us feel we cannot control our eating, but do we really try? If we know what we eat, why we eat, and how much we eat, that is the start of taking control of our habits.

Americans love to eat; 65 percent of all Americans are over-weight. What are you willing to sacrifice today to have a longer, healthier life? When we go overboard, we need to draft a plan (a life preserver, so to speak) giving ourselves a chance to make the changes needed to succeed. The foods we eat and how much we exercise help determine whether or not we will gain or lose weight. Weight management is an ongoing process that requires patience and diligence. We do not want to "diet." There is no such thing as a "diet." We have to man-age our weight for a lifetime. For the purposes of this book, the word "diet" will mean the food we eat for daily sustenance, not a short-term method to lose weight.

In order to succeed we must first believe
that we can.

Michael Korda

Foods contain mainly fats, carbohydrates, proteins, vitamins, and minerals. It is important to eat a balanced diet of all foods, and limit the amount of fat in the diet. (Refer to Factor Seven–Education for food groups and amounts of each.) Fats in the diet are essential for good health, but excess fat can contribute to heart disease, obesity, high blood pressure, some types of cancer, and other diseases like diabetes and gall stones.

The beginning is the most important part
of the work.

Plato

You need to monitor the foods you eat, and the calories and fat contained in that food so that you stay within a healthy budget of fat to calories. You want to eat no more than 20-30 percent fat on your budget to be healthy. That means that no more than 20-30 percent of your calories can come from fat. (The percent of fat is determined by multiplying the number of fat grams by nine, then dividing that number by the total calories consumed, times 100.) For example, for a total caloric intake of 1200 calories that includes 27 grams of fat:

27 grams x 9 = 243
243 ÷ 1200 = .2025
.2025 x 100 ≈ (20%)

"I can't do the math," you may cry! That's okay; see the chart below to determine your "fat allowance" for the day.

1200 calories.....................27-40 grams of fat/day
1500 calories.....................33-50 grams of fat /day
1700 calories.....................38-57 grams of fat/day
2000 calories.....................44-67 grams of fat/day
2250 calories.....................50-75 grams of fat/day
2500 calories.....................56-83 grams of fat/day

"Great...now I have to figure out how many calories to eat," you exclaim! Don't fear...help is here. Read on.

The American College of Sports Medicine recommends that healthy adults eat no fewer than 1200 calories per day.

Determine what your total caloric intake for the day should be. A good rule of thumb is to eat 10 calories for every pound of body weight to maintain that weight. So if you weigh 120 pounds, you need to eat 1200 calories (120 x 10 = 1200) to <u>maintain</u> your weight of 120 pounds. In order to lose one pound of weight, you have to consume and/or exercise off 3500 fewer calories. Once you have determined your normal caloric intake for one day, you can decide how many fewer calories per day you will eat (and still be healthy) to lose that pound of weight. Remember that you should only lose 1-2 pounds per week. (Losing one or two pounds a week should be a piece of cake! Sorry, maybe I shouldn't mention cake.) If you cut your caloric intake and increase exercise drastically, you may lose weight too quickly. You probably can't imagine losing weight too quickly; in fact, you probably think you can't lose it fast enough!

As crazy as it may seem, you can lose weight too quickly. You see, the reason is founded in how the body metabolizes food. It is physiologically impossible to lose more than about 1.6 pounds of fat mass per week. If you lose more than that, your body has to go somewhere to get the necessary energy, so you begin to lose lean body mass, otherwise known as muscle! The goal is to lose excess fat mass and increase lean body mass, not lose it! So, lose the excess pounds in fat mass by moderating your eating, and increase lean body mass through resistance training exercise. In fact, it is possible to be on a good weight management program and when you step on the scale, you see very little weight loss. What's up with that? You have to realize that the scale only tells you if your weight goes up or down. It does not tell you if you are losing inches, if you are losing fat mass or lean body mass, and it does not tell you if your clothes are fitting better! So do not be too dependent on the scale to measure your success or failure!

A pound of muscle burns 20 times more calories than a pound of fat.

When budgeting your calories, it might be helpful to think in the same terms as you will when budgeting your expenses.

Committed Food Expenses
(what you must consume to survive):
Bread, rice, cereal group
Vegetable group
Fruit group
Milk, yogurt, and cheese (dairy) group
Meat, poultry, fish, dry beans, nuts (protein) group
Water

Discretionary Food Expenses
(what you consume just because you like it):

fats: oils, butter, etc.	*alcohol*
ice cream	*French fries*
cookies	*fried chicken*
cakes	*fast food*
pastries	*doughnuts*

Caloric Expenses
(types of exercise to burn calories):

walking	*resistance exercise*
running	*weight training*
spinning	*yoga*
kick boxing	*versa-climber*
treadmill	*cycling*
water aerobics	*stairclimber*
cross country skiing	*rowing*

In addition, make sure you balance intake and expenditure of calories. Decide how many calories you can eat per day with the amount of time you spend exercising. (One minute of aerobic exercise within your target heart rate burns approximately 6 calories; 30 minutes of aerobics per day will burn about 180 calories!)

Whatever you want, do it now. There are only so many tomorrows.

Michael Landon

You can eat the things you like, but moderation is the key. That is, if you want to eat a piece of cake, do it. Don't deprive yourself. Either exercise more or eat fewer calories and fat at your next meal to "balance" the fat and calories of the cake. If you deprive yourself of your favorite foods, you will have more of a tendency to binge when you are tempted. Allow yourself to eat the things you enjoy, but eat them in moderation and be sure to "balance the budget." Planning a weekly menu will allow you to make healthy food choices and eat the things you like.

It can be done. I have a friend who has decided to live a healthy lifestyle. If she wants to go to her favorite hamburger joint, she "budgets" her calories, fat intake, and exercise that day so she can eat that big, juicy hamburger guilt free and still stay within her budget! It just takes a little planning.

✎ Activity

· ·

Now look back at your journal activity you did earlier in discussing this factor. Examine your journal record. Now:

- Determine what you ate because you were hungry, and what you ate because of your appetite.

- Make a list of your favorite foods and decide how you can moderate your choices.

- Decide what you can cut out and replace with something healthier.

- Make a menu for a week for each meal. Try to include appropriate food choices.

- Clear out your cupboards of "bad food".

- Make a shopping list of "good food" based on your menu choices.

- Make a list of the activities you enjoy. Determine which of those activities you can do for exercise to burn calories.

- Keep a daily food and exercise journal. Write down all the food that you eat, the number of calories and fat grams contained in the food, and the amount of exercise that you do. Do this every day.

Ask yourself these questions:

1. Am I eating more than 20-30 percent fat in my daily intake of food?

2. Do I regularly dine out for lunch/dinner?

3. Do I eat to satisfy my hunger or my appetite?

4. Am I eating only the minimum amount of calories necessary to maintain my weight?

5. Do I regularly eat things on impulse?

6. Am I exercising?

7. Do I include activities I enjoy in my exercise routines?

8. Am I making a shopping list of "good" food?

9. When I go to the grocery store, do I buy food on impulse, or do I stick to my menu plan?

10. Am I keeping my daily journal?

A common misconception is that a food budget is a diet. If you think of a food budget as only a list of what you eat, it won't work for you, because diets don't work over the long term. Think of a food budget as a device that gives you the information you need to make the most intelligent decisions about what you eat and how much you exercise. The way to ensure your budget is to regulate the caloric intake and energy expenditures. You need to be in control, and a good budget will put you there. Think of it as a tool that will help you become that mental picture of yourself!

> *Only actions give to life its strength, and only moderation gives it its charm.*
> Jean Paul Richter

Factor

Budget

Wealth

Husband to wife: "What do you say we take this money we've been saving toward a new car and blow it on a movie?"

The secrets of wealth building are practical and universal. They can be taught, and anyone can learn them and profit from them.

If you really want to be rich; if you want to have more wealth than your parents or peers, you have to start a long-term program. It won't happen overnight; wealth accumulation is an exercise in patience.

Patience Is A Virtue

Your current and potential income both influence just how much you can invest.

The first step is to *pay yourself first.*

Money
They call it legal tender,
That green and lovely stuff.
It's tender when you have it.
But when you don't it's tough!

A part of everything you own should be yours to keep. Before you pay others, put aside money for yourself.

You deserve to be a priority in your life. Give yourself a bonus, a reward for all the hard work you do. Believe in your ability to go for the gold!

This money is for your long-term wealth accumulation. It's not money for an emergency or short-term savings to purchase a large consumer item such as a car or boat. This is the foundation of your wealth pyramid. You can increase your portfolio without a lucrative job or huge business by properly using your current stream of income and the following strategies for budgeting.

Strategies for budgeting:

- *Record every penny you spend for the next month. You can do it. Start today and use your journal.*

- *Organize your spending into categories that make sense to you. Even though someone might not understand your strategies, you really do have a reason for the money you're spending.*

Investments You May Have Available:

IRA   401(k)

Pension Plans   Other Asset Purchases

Committed Expenses–Determine What Applies To You:

Housing   Prescription Drugs

Transportation   Care for Dependents

Education   Repayment of Loans

Insurance   Repayment of Charges

Food   Business Meals and Travel

Clothing   Alimony

Phone   Personal Care

Medical   Dry Cleaning

Discretionary Expenses–Money You Choose To Spend For Quality Of Life:

Entertainment   Dining

Vacation   Recreation/Club

Gifts   Hobbies

Long-Term Goals   Home Improvement

Miscellaneous

The above is just an example; add your own items if needed. Organize your spending into categories that *make sense to you.*

Budgets, of course are only estimates. When you are working with figures as large as Government figures of income and expense, differences between estimates and actual performance can easily arise... Balancing this budget is not simply a bookkeeping exercise or a businessman's fetish. It is the very keystone of financial responsibility.

George M. Humphrey

You should save 10 percent of your income if you are in your 20s or 30s. The higher your age and income, the higher percentage you should save. Start by saving 10 percent of the money in your wallet each week.

Make those little sacrifices; you will find that you won't even miss them! Over time, small amounts compound and you will find more and more money to save. You will get excited watching that money grow, and you will be more secure in your ability to handle an unexpected expense. Work toward saving 10 percent of your gross income a year.

If you save 10 percent a year, at the end of a decade you will have a full year's income saved before counting the money you put away for investments.

Wouldn't you love to be able to save 10 percent of your income? Well, of course you would, and you can do it!

Take a deep breath, and start compiling records of your spending for the past year or so. Sort through all of your checking statements and credit card bills. I know it sounds like a lot of work, but *"if it's worth doing, it's worth doing right!"* If you cannot find some needed paperwork, your bank or credit card company will provide backup copies of statements.

Once you have determined where you have spent your money, start to trim down the discretionary expenses.

Here are some ideas:

- *Cut one trip to a fast food restaurant.*

- *Serve one "frugal" meal a week.*

- *Stay at home one day a week.*

- *Use store brands instead of name brands.*

- *Use store and product coupons.*

- *Before you buy that item, whether it's clothes or merchandise, ask yourself if you really need it, and if not, put it back.*

- *Try going to the library or a second-hand bookstore instead of buying a new book.*

- *Use your journal; add additional areas you feel you can save. Share those additional ideas with a friend.*

It's not rocket science. You would be surprised how much of a cushion of spare change can be accumulated over time just by cutting back what you spend! Once you have started, you will find yourself continuing to think of different, new ways to save. Remember to set realistic goals. Check your journal occasionally to remind yourself where to save.

The second step of the process is to *control your expenditures.*

People feel that they can't save money, but do they really try? Do you know where you spend your money? If we implement a budget, it is easier to maintain the same standard of living as before we set up our budget.

It's not the big expenses that hurt us; it's the little ones.

Americans want instant gratification. Oh, yes you do—don't deny it. It's hard to say no to ourselves. Instead of giving into temptation, we should ask ourselves: "Is this something I *need*, or would I rather sacrifice today to have substantial assets that can be acquired later with accumulated savings?"

If overused credit cards are keeping you from feeling capable of getting started, don't feel alone. Americans have more credit card debt today then ever. Those who have gone overboard with debt should draft a plan giving creditors 20 percent of their income. Then, 70 percent of income should be used for living expenses. This may mean a lower standard of living for a while, but it also will mean a debt-free future that will be accompanied by a growing portfolio. **IT CAN BE DONE!**

✎ Activity

. . . .

- Cash expenditures can be difficult to track, which is why you need to use your journal to write down where you spend your money every day for at least three months.

- Separate expenditures by category.

- To determine if an expense is necessary, ask yourself: "Did I need the item or want the item?"

- Ask yourself, "How did I feel when I bought the item: happy, sad, depressed?"

Ask yourself these questions:

1. Am I spending more than 15 percent of my after-tax income on non-mortgage debt?

2. Do I regularly charge ordinary expenses on my credit cards?

3. Am I using cash advances from one card to pay off monthly balances on other credit cards?

4. Am I paying only the minimum amount due on my credit cards?

5. Have I tried to borrow money from friends and/or relatives?

6. Do I regularly purchase things on impulse?

7. Does my daily mail include past-due notices?

8. Am I getting new loans or extensions to pay off debts?

9. Am I using savings to pay bills I used to pay through my checking account?

10. Am I tapping into my life insurance cash value to pay monthly bills?

11. Do I depend on overtime to make ends meet each month?

12. Am I depending on checking account float or overdraft protection to pay monthly bills?

If you think of a budget as only a list of where you spend your money, it won't work for you. Think of it as device that gives you the information you need to make the most intelligent decisions. The way to ensure your budget is to regulate the expenses you are watching. You need to be in control, and a good budget will put you there. Think of it as a tool that will help you function better.

Factor 7

Education

> *The purpose of life is to live it, to reach out eagerly and without fear for newer and richer experience.*
>
> *Eleanor Roosevelt*

Factor

Education

Weight

Did you know that:

- *The strongest muscle in the body is the tongue?*

- *It is impossible to sneeze with your eyes open?*

- *Americans on the average eat 18 acres of pizza every day?*

- *Every time you lick a stamp, you are consuming 1/10 of a calorie?*

- *Two-thirds of the world's eggplant is grown in New Jersey?*

We live in the information age. The above "tidbits" were sent via an e-mail. The origin is unknown, but hopefully they are true! With so much information readily available, how do we know what is true or false? We have to get as much information as possible, learn as much as possible, and then make decisions based on the information. Every day we hear of new "diets" that promise weight loss without the hassle. Someday, science may actually discover the "magic bullet" that will safely make us fit and healthy overnight. For now, there is no easy fix. Most of us know that weight management is not easy. If it were easy, there would be no need for weight management programs, or for that matter, this book! We live in the information age and have the knowledge needed to be successful at our fingertips. Too often we envision ourselves as looking like the models in magazines. Society places much value on being thin, but being too thin can be as risky as being overweight. We have to take the knowledge that we have, expand on it, and put it into practice. A healthy body is the most important factor.

Promise and then perform.
Unknown

We know that weight management takes time, and that even though it is very individualized, there are certain principles that hold true across the board. Each individual has to learn what works for him or her. Some people may want to lose weight, others may want to increase muscle mass, and some people just want to maintain their present weight and physical fitness. Some people may be able to lose weight by just cutting down the portion sizes, and others need to count calories and/or grams of fat (refer to recipe box strategies). It is up to each person to evaluate his or her own needs and choose the methods that work.

Decide what is worthwhile and follow
through on it.
Unknown

There are nutrition basics that everyone should know before embarking on a weight management program. The nutrients in food are necessary to maintain a healthy lifestyle, and we need all types of food to insure the proper nutrition and energy for our activities and healthy bodies.

Many people are familiar with the basic food groups. Even though there is discussion about these groups and how much of each should be eaten, we need all of the basic groups to be healthy.

The U.S. Department of Agriculture and Department of Health and Human Services recommends the following servings from the food groups per day:

Bread, cereal, rice, and pasta group............4-11 servings

Fruit group..2-4 servings

Vegetable group..3-5 servings

Milk, yogurt, and cheese group..................2-3 servings

Meat, poultry, fish, dry beans,
eggs, and nuts group..................................2-3 servings

Fats, oils and sweets................................use sparingly

In addition, calories provide fuel for our bodies.
Carbohydrates are needed for quick energy. The body needs carbohydrates, because they are the primary fuel for muscles and the only fuel for the brain. We get carbohydrates from foods such as breads, fruits, vegetables, etc.

Proteins, which come from meat, fish, nuts, eggs, etc., are needed for muscle growth and to fuel endurance events.

Fats are fuel for low intensity exercise like walking. They fuel endurance events for about 90 minutes, and muscle uses fatty acids for fuel. One important thing to understand is that each gram of fat contains 9 calories, and each gram of protein and carbohydrates contains only 4 calories. That is one of the reasons that it is important to eat fats sparingly. Also, muscle mass burns many times more calories at rest than fat mass.

A balanced diet should provide all the necessary nutrients, but that is not always the case. Nutritional supplements aid in the dietary process when we do not get enough nutrients from the food we eat. We need vitamins and minerals for healthy bodies, and research has shown some supplements to be effective in preventing certain diseases.

A little neglect may breed great mischief...
...for want of a nail, the shoe was lost; for
want of a shoe, the horse was lost; for want
of a horse, the rider was lost.
                                        Ben Franklin

Not only is it important to eat a balanced diet, but good nutrition also includes the often overlooked but important component...water. It is recommended that you drink eight glasses of water per day.

Water is a commonly overlooked endurance aid. Proper exercise performance is dependent on proper hydration. Proper fluid intake will help prevent dehydration. If you get dehydrated, the heart rate increases, the blood flow to the skin decreases, and the body temperature increases. This puts you at risk for heat exhaustion and/or heat stroke.

If you are exercising in hot conditions, it is recommended that you drink 2-3 glasses of water 1 1/2 - 2 hours before exercise, 4-8 ounces for every 10-20 minutes of exercise, and then another 1-2 glasses after exercise. If conditions vary, you can moderate the amount of water, but you should still drink before, during and after exercise.

Exercise plays a large role in a successful weight loss plan. Through exercise, we use calories and possibly gain muscle mass. Exercise has also been shown to increase bone density. Exercise is an integral part of the weight loss equation. It has been found that people who exercise regularly are less likely to develop cancer than those who do not. Weight bearing exercise helps increase bone density, and resistance exercise helps increase muscle mass. Muscle needs more calories to fuel it than does fat, so the more muscle mass we have, the more calories we can burn, thus affecting our metabolism. As earlier discussed, fluid replacement is very important before, during, and after exercise.

Tomorrow's life is too late. Live today.
Martial

We have the knowledge base, and yet 65 percent of Americans are overweight. This statistic suggests that people are ignoring the basics (i.e., eating a balanced diet, exercising, and working toward a healthy lifestyle). If the education system has not taught enough people the basics, then it's up to them to teach themselves how to achieve a healthy life.

---

*The beautiful thing about learning is that
nobody can take it away from you.*
B.B. King

There is no short cut to a healthy weight loss plan, but step by step you can improve your eating and exercise habits. It takes work and the time to educate yourself.

Where to begin?

The Federal Government has many free publications available. This is unbiased information based on research. Check your public library for information on the Internet.

Those who can afford it might try hiring a personal trainer. Be careful, however: not all trainers are equally qualified. Look for a trainer who is certified by a reputable organization. If you are not comfortable with a particular person, find someone else.

1. Start by asking friends or family members if they are working with anyone and get a referral.

2. Interview several prospects.

3. Ask how they are compensated. (Some personal trainers are paid by the hour; others offer package deals for a certain number of sessions.) It doesn't matter how they are paid; depending on your needs, choose the compensation method that best suits you.

4. Ask if they work with others in your same age group and circumstances.

5. Ask for names of clients to call; ask if they are happy with the work the trainer has done for them.

When educated, you will understand that all weight loss programs are not safe and effective, and there are many different types of programs. Find the one that "fits" the best for you.

I'm on a "see"food diet. I eat everything I see!
Anonymous

There are many weight management programs. Some programs are well-known and have been very successful in helping people lose weight. Avoid fad diets that do not promote a balanced diet. Many of the high protein diets are questionable not only because of the long-term effects of remaining on the diet, but because when the human body is deprived of carbohydrates, it acts as if it is starving. Since the body needs carbohydrates and it is not getting them from the food, the body does the only thing it can: it tries to get the needed energy to fuel the muscles and the brain from itself. First it uses the meager amount of stored carbohydrates, then your body goes after stored protein (muscle) and then stored fat.

Remember that there is no such thing as a "diet." You must commit to a change in eating and exercise habits as discussed in the previous factors to be successful for the rest of your life.

Be patient: successful weight management depends on discipline and determination. Once you have an understanding of weight management strategies that are best for you, you can start a weight management program based on your time frame, goals, and objectives.

For everything that you have missed,
you have gained something else.
Emerson

Getting back to the basics of weight loss:

- *There's no time like the present. Don't put it off; do it today!*

- *It's never too late to start.*

- *It may be hard to teach an old dog new tricks, but it's possible.*

- *It's not timing the weight loss; it's allowing enough time for the weight loss.*

There are certain steps you must take to maintain control.

Don't put all of your eggs in one basket. Don't rely on dieting alone or exercise alone for your weight management program. A combination of the two works best.

Take control of your lifestyle. Stay involved and aware of what you eat, when you eat it, and why you eat it. Don't forget to be realistic in your goals and your time frame. Make good food choices and remember to budget your choices. If you develop a sensible, disciplined, and most importantly, consistent approach to weight management, you will live a healthier lifestyle. Exercise regularly.

Don't drive yourself crazy. Acknowledge that there will be days when you will overeat or not exercise enough. That is okay. Just make sure that the next day you are careful about what you eat and resume exercising. Occasionally it is good to take a day or two off from exercising to give your body a chance to recover. Don't be too hard on yourself. Focus your energy on consistent strategies for a healthy lifestyle.

He who tastes not, knows not.
Unknown

✎ Activity

• •

- Evaluate your current weight, level of exercise, and lifestyle.

- List the areas you need to address, then list the action steps for the changes that need to be made.

- Determine what steps need to be taken to educate yourself and to improve your plan.

Keep in mind the common mistakes made when attempting weight management:

- Trying to lose too much weight too fast.

- Going on fad diets.

- Trying to use diet alone to control weight instead of a combination of diet and exercise.

- Making inappropriate food choices.

- Making emotional decisions.

- Having unrealistic expectations.

- Having the misconception that being thin means being healthy.

- Using the scale as the only measure of success.

- Not exercising.

> *With education, it's a dream anyone can manage.*
>
>   *Unknown*

Factor 7

Education

Wealth

Money isn't everything, and don't let anybody tell you it is. There are other things, such as stocks, bonds, letters of credit, travelers' checks, and drafts.

Financial security: For the average working person, security brings to mind images of endless days on sunny beaches, or perhaps the assurance that the dividend check is in the mail.

Reality Sucks! While many of us spend our time dreaming of financial independence, according to two recent surveys, most Americans lack the education and skills necessary to reach their elusive goal.

For example, the College of Financial Planning, a Denver institution that trains financial planners, found that:

- About 73 percent of Americans don't set financial goals.

- 65 percent don't save enough.

- 61 percent don't budget their income.

According to the 2003 Retirement Confidence Survey:

- Nearly 24 percent of workers age 45 or older this year (2003) say they plan to postpone their retirement age— up 9 percentage points from 2002 (15 percent), mainly due to financial or econmic concerns.

- Both workers and retirees say they spent more time planning for the holidays (74 percent) and social events (57 percent) than they did for retirement (49 percent).

- Even scarier, 17 percent surveyed spent no time planning for retirement.

These statistics show that people are ignoring the basics (i.e., budgeting, saving and retirement planning) because their education system does not teach these basics. Therefore, it's up to them to teach themselves how to achieve their financial security.

Don't let what you cannot do interfere with what you can do.

John Wooden

There is no shortcut to financial security. Step by step, you can improve money-management skills, but it takes work and the time to educate yourself. Yes, I said **WORK** and **TIME!**

Where do you begin?

Many libraries and bookstores have financial magazines. The articles are easy to understand and can be applied to almost any household.

Check the paper; there are many seminars and workshops available. I would go to as many as possible. You will find that you will learn something new each time you go. If the seminars are free, you might be expected to listen to a sales pitch. Don't let that keep you from attending and getting the information.

Those who can afford it might try hiring a financial planner. Be careful, however, as not all planners are equally qualified. Ask lots of questions before you let anyone invest your money or offer you advice. And if you are not comfortable with a particular person, find someone else.

1. Start by asking a friend or family member if they are working with anyone, and get a referral.

2. Interview several prospects.

3. Ask how they are compensated. (Some financial planners receive a fee, others receive a commission.) It doesn't matter how they are paid; everyone has to make a living. Depending on your needs, choose the compensation method that best suits you.

4. Ask if they work with others in your same age group and circumstances.

5. Ask for names of clients to call and ask if they are happy with the work the planner has done for them.

People tend to procrastinate, and many fail because they are comfortable in their ignorance. They feel that it would be too confusing, too hard, or take too much time. Some just don't realize there is a problem until it's too late, and if you don't realize there's a problem, how can you deal with it?

Through education, you will understand that saving is not the same as investing. Although you have to be able to save to invest, if your "investment" doesn't fluctuate with the market, it's not an investment, it's a savings account.

Rome wasn't built in a day!

Be patient: successful investors are disciplined and patient. Once you have an understanding of investment strategies, you can invest based on your time frame, goals, and objectives. When you have a long-term time frame, you will not overreact to the market fluctuation that history has proven you will surely experience. Instead, you will understand that proper diversification of your assets will allow you to reap the reward of higher returns.

Death and taxes are two of life's certainties that affect your financial planning. In addition, count on inflation rearing its ugly head. Inflation is very tenacious.

It continually erodes away your purchasing power. When projecting how much money you will need to achieve your financial goals, you must factor in the impact of inflation on living costs.

For example, assuming an inflation factor of 4.5 percent per year, what you pay in those expenses will be doubled in 15 years. If you are 50 years old, you might estimate that if you were to retire today, you would need $20,000 in personal investment income (in addition to other sources of income like Social Security and your company pension). Actually, when calculated, you would need a higher income when you retire in order to have the same *"purchasing power"* that $20,000 has today. In fact, if living costs double every fifteen years, you will need to double your money, or $40,000, in investment income when you reach the age of 65.

Activity is the only road to knowledge.
George Bernard Shaw

Getting back to the basics of investing:

- *There's no time like the present. Procrastination is the number one money mistake.*

- *It's never too early to start. (The sooner you start, the greater your chances are for success, with less money).*

- *It's never too late to start. (However, the later you start, the more money you will have to invest for additional years).*

- *It may be hard to teach an old dog new tricks, but it's possible.*

- *It's not timing the market; it's time in the market.*

Once the basics are taken care of, your next step is the management of your investments. Whether you manage your own investments or hire someone to do it for you, make the most of your investments.

> You cannot cross the sea merely by standing
> and staring at the water.
> R. Tagore

There are certain steps you must take to maintain control.

Don't put all of your eggs in one basket. Spread your investment into various types of securities.

Take control of your investments. Stay involved and keep up to date on what's happening. If you have someone working with you, be sure they know your risk tolerance, goals, and time frame. Have them explain where your money is and what your expectations should be. Know if your investments are appropriate for you. If you develop a sensible, disciplined, and most importantly, consistent approach to investing, you can be your own best investment advisor. Also, you can ask the right questions and receive the most important answers from your advisor.

Keep an eye on what's happening. Consistent monitoring of your investments unfortunately takes some time, but you will find that it's worth the time. Keep up to date on the market conditions. It will be time well spent!

Don't drive yourself crazy. If you are a new investor, you will be tempted to track your investments too often and that can easily become an obsession. Focus your energy on well-respected publications and information from the companies in which you have invested.

Where do you find the information you need?

Annual Reports

Usually free, it is the company's summary statement about what has happened in the past, present and the most recent financials.

Analyst's Recommendations

There are a bevy of analysts who produce numerous reports on particular companies, industries, mutual funds, and the economy in general.

Standard & Poors

The S&P is a wonderful source for bond and stock reports. Available at larger public and university libraries, you can get substantial history and current performances of thousands of stocks.

Moody's Investors Services

Like S&P, Moody's is an invaluable source of information by professionals and nonprofessionals alike. Again, it lists substantial company data that you can use to determine the health of a particular investment choice. Like the S&P, Moody's should be available at larger public libraries.

Financial Magazines

Financial magazines are a dime a dozen. Many are specifically investor-oriented, while some focus on the overall market, business and what's happening to the economy. *Money, Forbes, Business Week, Kiplinger's Worth, Financial World,* etc.

On-line Information

If you have access to a computer, you have an unending source of information available to you.

Learn to reason forward and backward and on all sides of the question.

Unknown

✎ Activity

....

- Evaluate your current portfolio holdings.

- List the areas you need to address, then list the action steps for the changes that need to be made.

- Determine what steps need to be taken to educate yourself, and to improve your plan.

- Regularly monitor your portfolio allocation and performance.

Keep in mind the common mistakes investors make:

- Investing too conservatively.

- Forgetting it's not timing the market, but time in the market.

- Making quick decisions, without regard to the consequences.

- Making inappropriate investment choices.

- Lacking a clear understanding of taxes.

- Making emotional decisions.

- Maintaining too many investment accounts.

- Not seeking professional help

Factor

Goals

> *When what we are is what we*
> *want to be, that's happiness.*
> *Malcolm Forbes*

Factor 8

Goals

Weight

It has been a bad day for Charlie Brown. He has struck out for the third straight time. In disgust, he says, "Rats!" Back in the dugout, he buries his face in his hands and laments to Lucy, "I'll never be a big-league ball player. All my life I've dreamed of playing in the big leagues, but I just know I'll never make it."

Lucy responds, "You're thinking way too far ahead, Charlie Brown. What you need are more immediate goals."

"Immediate goals?" asks Charlie Brown.

"Yes," says Lucy. "Start right now with this next inning. When you go out to pitch, see if you can walk out to the mound without falling down."
(from *The Speaker's Sourcebook*)

When you are starting any type of a weight management program, you should have certain realistic goals. How do you determine your goals?

In Factor Six–Budget–we discussed assessing where you are right now in terms of calories taken in and calories expended. We also touched on the fact that everyone has a certain amount of lean body mass and fat mass. The more fat we have, the higher our body's percent of fat. To become healthier and fit, we want to lose excess fat and increase lean body mass. Now you are going to take a good hard look at yourself and determine what you want to change. Deciding on the changes will assist you in setting your goals for good weight management.

Some think that when you are heavy, it is impossible to become what you believe is thin. It is also difficult to accept anything less than a weight that is probably impossible to achieve. Whoa! Stop right there! Are you just talking about losing weight? The amount on the scale is not the only thing that determines your size and fitness level! Adjust your thought process to think about weight management and increased health and fitness. Too many Americans are obsessed with looking like a model, and not being comfortable with their weight. Remember: you are starting a whole new lifestyle that you will continue forever, and the result will be a more fit, healthier you!

Make sure your goals are realistic. By setting unrealistic goals, you make it impossible to do anything, so you eat everything in sight and then hate yourself later. What's right for one person is not necessarily right for the next. I learned that for myself. I knew what was possible and I set my goals, based on my personal assessment.

Pursue worthy aims.

Solon

How do you figure out what you should look like? The first step is to look at yourself as you are <u>now</u>. Get in front of a mirror naked (Yikes!!!). That's right; strip down, and shake your body. Wherever you jiggle, you need to lose fat and replace it with lean body mass.

I know how I felt, and it was not a pretty sight! We don't usually look at ourselves closely, so make it a critical look. You also need to accept the fact that you will never be perfect, but you can be perfectly happy! There are certain aspects about you that can never be changed, no matter how much weight you lose. Your body type plays an important part in the process.

There are three body types as categorized by Dr. W. H. Sheldon:

1. The ectomorph is the person who is long and lanky.

2. The mesomorph is more rectangular or pear shaped with sturdy arms and legs.

3. The curvy endomorph is more rounded, tending toward the plump.

You probably fit into one of these categories. Remember that as long as you believe that losing weight is going to change your basic body shape, you have set yourself for failure and frustration.

When I was as my heaviest, I used to say, *"If only I were two feet taller, I would be the right size."* Well obviously, you can't change your height. Come to peace with the fact that the sooner you accept yourself, the more successful you will be.

One important thing to remember is to change the things you can. For example, you **CAN NOT** spot-reduce. How do you change those areas that you want to change? So many people will ask, "What exercise can I do to get rid of my fat stomach?" The answer is, "There is not one single exercise to flatten your stomach." Now that may sound discouraging, but it really isn't that bad.

There is no shortcut. Victory lies in overcoming obstacles every day.

Author unknown

In order to lose the fat in your stomach area, you have to engage in some form of aerobic activity to get rid of the fat. Since the word aerobic means "with or in the presence of oxygen," an aerobic activity is any activity that conditions the cardiovascular system by using movements that create an increased demand for oxygen over an extended period of time. You can do abdominal crunches to gain increased muscle in the area. The combination of sensible eating, aerobic exercise, resistance exercise and patience will lead to a flat stomach! Unfortunately, the part of your body where you want to lose the most fat and replace with muscle may be the last place you will see progress.

You see, some areas of the body are more stubborn and don't want to let go of the fat! These areas are called enzyme resistant. Areas that are enzyme resistant to losing fat in women are located in the hips and thighs and in men, in the abdominal region. (Bet you never would have guessed that!) Also, your family history will show you which areas will be more "stubborn." If your relatives have large hips and small waists, chances are you will experience the same body shape. Or if your family members tend to have rounded stomachs, you will find that your stomach is the last place to lose excess fat. It is important to learn which are your "trouble spots" and to be patient. Don't give up! Diligence will pay off in the end!

Set small goals and once reached, set additional small goals.

Don't be impatient: impatience is non-productive. If you have a lot of pounds to lose, develop the attitude that you are going to reduce in stages. If your goal is to lose one hundred pounds in two months, you are going to be very disappointed, but if you tell yourself that in one month you will lose five pounds, your chances are very good that you will succeed. Doctors say that if you can lose one pound a week, chances are you will keep it off.

If you lose five pounds each month, then you will lose sixty pounds in one year. If you want to lose three inches around your waist, your goal might be 1/4 inch a month, and all three inches will be gone in a single year!

Now think about how long you've been in the shape you're in. A month? A year? Many years? Have you been overweight all your life? Did something happen to cause the weight gain?

- *Did you go through a life-changing event? (Divorce, separation, loss of a loved one...)*

- *Did you put on weight during pregnancy and never took it off?*

- *Was your pregnancy five years ago, ten years ago?*

- *Did you put on weight when you stopped smoking? When did you stop smoking?*

- *Did you/do you exercise?*

- *What kind of exercise do you (or did you) do?*

When you decide on your goal, think about the above questions. If you took ten years to put on your weight, it is unrealistic to expect to take the weight off in a month.
Set small goals and once reached, set additional small goals.

To be what we are and to become what we are capable of becoming is the only end in life.
Robert Louis Stevenson

Remember that you are made up of lean body mass and fat mass. If you take the weight off too quickly, you will lose lean body mass as well as fat mass. Is that good weight management? The weight scale may go down, but is it the weight you want to lose? And do we always want the weight to go down? Weight management includes gaining muscle mass, which actually weighs more than fat mass! This is where exercise comes in. If we lose fat and increase muscle, we cannot just judge success by the weight on the scale. You could lose inches, but the scale will not tell you that! That is why you should take your measurements as well as check your weight! Make sure you take your measurements each month and record them in your journal so you can watch the inches shrink away!

Now, let's think about exercise goals. Successful weight management has to include some type of exercise. You should do some form of aerobic exercise 30 minutes at least three times a week, and do resistance training a minimum of two times a week.

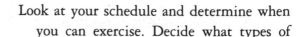

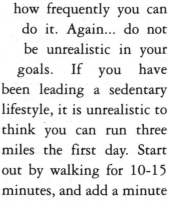

Look at your schedule and determine when you can exercise. Decide what types of exercise you enjoy doing and how frequently you can do it. Again... do not be unrealistic in your goals. If you have been leading a sedentary lifestyle, it is unrealistic to think you can run three miles the first day. Start out by walking for 10-15 minutes, and add a minute or two every few days. Start to jog for a minute or two in between several minutes of walking. Before you know it, you will be walking/jogging for 30 minutes a day without a break!

The same process holds true for resistance training. You don't have to join a gym and bench-press 150 pounds the first day there. Start at home by doing push-ups or using cans of food for weights. Slowly build up the weight, and maybe even buy some light (5,10,15 pound) hand weights to use. Fitness becomes a wonderful habit if you give it a chance! You can be a fit person!

✎ Activity

- Make a list of your realistic goals. Sit down with those individuals in your life that will affect your success in reaching those goals. Take into consideration:

- Am I satisfied with my body, my food intake, and my fitness level?

- Do I want to become healthier, have more energy, and enjoy life more?

- How much weight and/or inches do I want to lose or gain? (You might want to lose inches in your waist, but gain inches in your biceps!)

- How much do I exercise now, and how much can I do and be able to "stick with it?"

- In the activity for Factor Six–Budget, you kept track of your calories and amount of exercise. For this factor, make a daily schedule of how much time you plan to exercise and stick to it.

- Be specific: make sure you write down exactly what you want to accomplish.

- Be pro-active: focus on what action you need to take to succeed.

- Make it measurable: have a definite time frame for when your goal will be completed.

- Give yourself enough time: take small steps, and don't expect too much too soon.

- Have realistic expectations, and understand that obstacles may keep you from reaching your goals.

- Always write your goals down. If you don't, you will have a hard time knowing whether or not you've reached them.

- Use your journal everyday, and go back and read it occasionally to remind yourself where you've been and where you want to go.

- Now, write down your goals in your journal.
  For example:
  - I will lose ten pounds in the next three months.

  - When I have lost ten pounds, I will reward myself with a new sweater.

  - I will cut 300 calories out of my diet every day.

  - I will exercise for 20 minutes three times a week.

  - I will fit into my favorite pair of pants by Christmas.

Make sure to revisit your goals, and as you achieve your goals, write down new ones. If you did not achieve your goal, assess the reasons and make changes. Goal setting is an ongoing process. By taking small steps, you can overcome giant hurdles! You are the only one who can make a difference in your life. DO IT TODAY!

> *Make a success of living by seeing the*
> *goal and aiming for it unswervingly.*
> *Cecil B. DeMille*

Factor

Goals

Wealth

Bank customer to loan officer: "I just need enough to tide me over until I can figure out where to get some money."

I know sometimes we are overwhelmed by the fact that it takes money to make money, but we all have to start somewhere. Take one step at a time; you have to crawl before you can walk, walk before you can run, and run before you can sprint.

When you are starting to invest, you should have certain financial goals in mind. On the surface, the objective of most investors is to make money grow. How have you been planning to use the money, and when did you think you would need it? It all goes back to that time in your life when you first started investing, or maybe you are starting your investment strategies now. Were/are you planning to save for your first house, or maybe a vacation home? Was/is your child's education the priority, or a comfortable retirement at the top of your list?

Assessing Your Goals

You may not think so, but assessing your goals is simpler than it sounds. Take a minute to think about what your financial goals are right now. Would you like that new leather coat, new car, better apartment, new furniture? No matter what you desire, it is okay, you deserve it. Remind yourself daily of your goals as you're making your list. Use your journal.

Next, consider how much money you may need to achieve your goals, and how soon you will need it. Now you need to compare these goals to the **short-, medium-, and long-term** investment potential of your portfolio investments. If you have no investments, it's all right, you will. You are taking the steps to achieve a positive financial future.

Whatever you do, don't set objectives without pondering how you will meet them. You will not be doing yourself a favor if you make unrealistic decisions without thinking about how you will obtain that goal. Your goals need to be accompanied by actual *strategies* for attaining them.

Strategies for creating successful financial goals:
- Organize your finances.
- Look at the big financial picture, as well as individual goals.
- Figure out the cost of major financial goals.
- Pinpoint opportunities you may be missing.
- Find ways to reach each goal.

Because we all have to start somewhere, be careful to set modest goals at first. There will be plenty of time to take on more ambitious targets later. When you did your budget, you were able to determine where you spent your money. Take a close look at last year's spending, and look where you might change your spending dollars to meet the goals you have set for yourself.

In the long run, we only hit what we aim at.
Thoreau

Whether you're new at investing or you're a seasoned pro, it's important to periodically make sure your "aim is true" to achieve your financial goals.

Do not turn back when you are just at the goal.
Pubilius Syrus

Think about what you want. Obviously you can't set goals if you don't know your dreams, and when you write those dreams down they become goals.

Short-Term Goals Investment Options: (0 to 2 years)
Buying a new outfit, Getting your car fixed, Paying off your debt, Saving for a special occasion, Going on vacation:
- *CDs*
- *Money Market Accounts*
- *Passbook Savings Accounts*

Medium-Term Goals Investment Options: (2 to 5 years)
Buying a new car, Remodeling your home, Planning a vacation, Buying a new home, Sending teenager to college:

- *Short-Term Bonds*
- *High Grade Municipal Bonds*
- *Corporate Bonds*
- *Long-Term CDs*
- *Balanced Mutual Funds*
- *Preferred Stock*

Long-Term Goals Investment Options: (5 to ? years)
Buying a new home, Buying a vacation home, Saving for younger child's college, Saving for a really great vacation, Saving for your retirement:
- *Blue Chip Common Stock*
- *Growth and Income*
- *Growth*
- *Aggressive Growth*
- *Mutual Funds (Domestic, Global or International)*
- *Annuities*

If you start investing with nothing in mind, that's fine, but it often helps to set goals so you're conscious of the progress you're making and where you're headed financially.

Once you've set your goals, you need to revisit them every year. You may think of something really great to have! Sometimes changes occur so slowly that we are unaware of how they will affect the end result. It's important to recognize the realities of your changing goals and time horizons. If not, your portfolio could be delivering results that meet your expectations today, but fall short of your actual needs tomorrow.

Success comes before work only in the dictionary.
Anonymous

✎ Activity

•••

- Make a list of your goals. Sit down with those individuals in your life that will affect your success in reaching those goals. Prioritize goals in four categories:
  A. Essentials
  B. Strong Desire
  C. Would Like
  N/A   Not Applicable

- Once you determine the priority, establish how much you will need and your time frame.

- Be specific: make sure you write down exactly what you want to accomplish.

- Be pro-active: focus on what action you need to take to succeed.

- Make it measurable: establish a definite time frame of when your goal will be completed.

- Schedule enough time: take baby steps, and don't expect too much too soon.

- Develop realistic expectations and allow for obstacles to get in the way of your success.

- Use your journal to create a prioritized task list. Have a realistic finish time line. Cross off each item as you complete it.

Life can only disappoint you if you let it.
Mark Hopkins

Factor

Time

Factor

Time

Weight

Question: How do men exercise at the beach?
Answer: By sucking in their stomachs every time they see a bikini.

Everyone wants to look good, but few want to allow themselves the time to achieve their goals. It seems we are always looking for that "quick fix," rather than allowing enough time to manage our weight sensibly. Time plays an important part in the weight management process. There are several aspects of time to consider when developing a good weight management plan. Think about these things: How much time will it take for me to achieve my goal weight? How will I "mark" time to effectively manage my eating habits? How much time do I have to exercise?

Give yourself the gift of time. Keep in mind the amount of time it took you to put on your extra pounds. Realistically, it will take many months to take off the pounds sensibly and become a fit, healthier person, just as it took many months for you to put on weight and become unfit! Keep in mind that weight management is not just about weight loss. It is about becoming the fit person you can be, and feeling good about yourself!

Nothing astonishes others so much as common sense and plain dealing.
                                        Emerson

As stated before, doctors say that we should not lose more than a pound or two a week. In fact, studies have shown that it is physiologically impossible to lose more than 1.6 pounds of fat mass a week. That means that if you are losing more than about a pound and a half a week, you are actually losing fat free mass, or muscle! Losing muscle mass is counter-productive in a good weight management program.

If you want to lose one pound a week, you have to eat less and exercise more so that the eating less and exercising amounts to 500 fewer calories per day. (Remember: it takes 3,500 fewer calories to lose one pound of weight.) For example, if you cut your caloric intake by 250 calories, you must exercise enough to burn the other 250 calories. That amounts to 500 fewer calories per day, a reasonable goal to achieve!

So you may say, "Why not just eat half as much as I normally do and skip the exercise?" Keep in mind that you do not want to eat too few calories. If you do, your body may think that it is "starving" and may actually slow down its metabolism to keep you from "starving." Slowing down your metabolism is counter-productive to weight loss. You want to maintain a healthy balance of nutrition and exercise to keep your metabolism burning those calories!

1. Decide what weight management program you will use. Will you do it on your own? Will you join a structured program? (See discussion of weight loss programs in Factor Seven–Education and Factor Twelve–Risk.) Always consult your doctor before starting any weight management program.

2. Determine the amount of weight and/or inches you want to lose or gain.

3. Break those amounts down into reasonable goals. Give yourself enough time to achieve your goals.

Take the time to use your journal to write down what time of day you eat. There are usually times of day that we tend to overeat. When you eat is as important as what you eat. Breakfast, in the opinion of most nutritionists, is the most important meal, yet it is often the most "forgotten" meal. Breakfast can get your metabolism into high gear! Don't neglect a good breakfast! By the same token, heavy eating just before bed is not a good idea because your metabolism slows down when you sleep.

Begin to take control of time by strictly adhering to whatever food plan you choose. Your menus designate mealtimes as well as meal selections. When you stick to your menus day after day and week after week, you are not just forming new habits over time, but you are learning a control technique.

---

*Do the little things well now. In time,
great things will be presented to you,
waiting to be done.*
                              Persian proverb

The idea of marking time by numbers is to make it seem to go faster. However, we don't want the time of becoming healthy and fit to ever come to an end. For this reason, the first phase of your weight management program should be very simple, so you can take control of your eating habits. Cut down on calories, exercise more, but don't deprive yourself of everything you enjoy! Establish your weight management "budget" and give yourself time to establish new patterns and habits so you can achieve success!

---

*You should punish your appetites rather
than allow your appetites to punish you.*
                              Epcitetus

Time is one of the most focused-on aspects of weight management. Most "dieters" think adhering to a controlled eating regimen in terms of Day 1, Day 2 or Week 3, and so on, and literally count the passing time like a prison sentence. They can not wait until the end of their "sentence" so they can be released and go back to their old habits! Don't let that happen to you! You are not on a "diet" and there is not an end to your new lifestyle. You must think of your total weight management program as a lifetime commitment, not just a diet. Remember: time is on your side!

Choose a day of the month that you will measure yourself. Decide which areas you want to measure. Use that same day and time of every month to take the measurements. Record your measurements each month in your journal: this will give you a sense of what you have accomplished. Small decreases in these measurements make a huge difference in your size! You might be surprised how much difference 1/4" can make! You will have to admit that as the measurements decrease, you feel great! Sometimes, though, the measurements begin to increase. When this happens, it sends an alert message that you had better evaluate your program and make decisions based on where you want to be! The scale is not the only tool to help you "measure" your success.

You will also want to weigh yourself once a month, at the same time of day, on the same scale, and preferably with no clothes. Record your weight in your journal. By only weighing yourself once a month, you give yourself time to see the effect of your program. Weighing yourself daily can be a frustrating experience. Your weight can fluctuate from 1-3 pounds a day due to fluid retention, otherwise known as "water weight." Remember that factors that influence your changing body weight are not consistent.

These factors include:

- *How much fluid retention or loss in your body on any given day. (1-3 pounds per day can be normal reaction to amount of fluid.)*

- *How much you weigh before you start your weight loss program.*

- *How sluggish your metabolism is and how quickly it adjusts to a reduction in calories and nutritionally balanced meals.*

- *Your body's own pattern of weight loss (these patterns differ from person to person and between males and females).*

- *The chemical processes, many of which are not yet fully understood, that make up the metabolism.*

Now that you have given yourself enough time to gain control and start change, you are probably thinking about exercise, and how you do not have enough time in the day to do everything now! You should exercise aerobically for a minimum of 3-5 times a week for 30 minutes, and do resistance (weight) training 3 times a week.

"How can I possibly find time to exercise?" you ask.
There is not an easy answer to that question. You have to decide that exercise is worth the commitment. Once you make the commitment, decide where you can "find" the time to exercise. Here are some suggestions:

- *Walk to the workplace if at all possible.*

- *Use the stairs instead of the elevator or escalator.*

- *Replace one 30-minute TV show with exercise. Better yet, exercise while watching your favorite show! Use an exercise bike; rowing, step, or ski machine; jump rope, etc.*

- *Do abdominal crunches while watching TV.*

- *Actually schedule an exercise time on your calendar or in your planner. Make exercise a commitment.*

- *Take your dog for a walk every day.*

- *Go for a walk with your friend, spouse, family member, etc., after dinner...not only will you exercise, but you will also spend time with the people you care about!*

Record all time spent exercising in your journal. You can even create graphs for each month to illustrate the time spent. It will give you a great feeling!

Time is on your side. After spending time at the chopping block, weighing all the factors of your weight management program and recording your weight, measurements, and time spent exercising, continue to use your journal to record when and what you eat, how you feel when you're eating, and why you're eating. You will gain a better understanding of yourself.

Church Bulletin Blooper: Jean will be leading a weight-management series Wednesday nights. She's used the program herself and has been growing like crazy!

✎ Activity

• •

- Develop your time frame based on your goals.

- Set realistic objectives based on those time frames.

- Set a time to weigh yourself.

- Set a time to measure yourself.

- Schedule a time to exercise.

- Use your journal to record your weight, measurements, and time spent exercising from month to month. (Some health clubs have computer programs that keep track of your exercise, calories used, etc. See if your club has one!)

It takes time to be a success, but time is all it takes.

Unknown

Factor

Time

Wealth

If you had to retire tomorrow, would you be ready? Do you tell yourself, "Relax, I have plenty of *time* before I retire"? Just because this may appear to be true, it does not mean this perception could not be a problem. Too many of us talk about retirement as if it were so far away that we don't take a serious look at it today.

Even if you're not close to retiring, what is your time frame? What if you had to retire in five to ten years? Do you know what you need to live comfortably? What ordinary living expenses and monthly debt would you have to pay from your income sources at retirement?

There are just a few income possibilities:

1. Social Security

2. Employer-sponsored Retirement Plans (Pension 401(k) plans, Thrift Savings plans)

3. Personal Assets (Individual Retirement Accounts)

4. Government Pensions

5. Accumulated Assets (Savings, Individual accounts, Annuities)

Will your income from the above sources meet your needs? And if so, for how long?

As you may know, the future of Social Security is uncertain.

How will the future of Social Security affect your future?

Like many investors, you may be counting on a number of sources for financial support during your retirement. The future of Social Security has many people feeling uncertain about their own future. The basic situation is this: without reform to the present system, it is predicted that Social Security benefits being paid out will exceed the revenues coming in from employed workers as early as 2013, and Social Security will have used up its huge accumulated surplus by the year 2030.

The government is considering several plans to avoid disaster while keeping the basic safety net of Social Security intact. Possible solutions range from initiating private savings through individual investment accounts, to giving the government the power to invest some of the money in stocks.

To add to the uncertainty, many companies are reducing the emphasis placed on traditional pension plans provided to employees. In this environment, it's important to plan carefully

and make the most of the
time and the personal
retirement savings you
control.

Until the
appropriate
course of
action is
approved,
the government is
encouraging taxpayers to take on more individual responsibility for retirement savings and earnings. For example, the
Department of Labor has issued guidelines to help companies
better educate employees about their 401(k) options. And
there's also been bipartisan support for expanding IRA contributions and giving employees at small companies easier access
to pensions.

Given the uncertain conditions of Social Security, there may
never be a better time to sit down and determine what you can
do to make sure your retirement is secure.

Distance tests a horse's strength. . . time
reveals a man's character.

                                    Chinese proverb

This is where the power of tax-deferred investments such as
IRAs becomes clear. IRAs shelter your contributions and all of
their earnings–including their dividends and capital
gains–from taxes until withdrawal. This means that 100

percent of your investment and its accumulated earnings are working for you.

Tax-deferred investments can give you an incredible advantage over taxable investment options. Time is important when deciding to invest in a tax-deferred plan. Remember, this is a long-term retirement plan, and money needed before age 59 1/2 could be penalized.

As you can see, tax-deferred investments can certainly help you reach your retirement goals, and when you combine them with the benefit of time, you can increase your advantage. While it may never be too late to start saving for retirement, the sooner you begin investing, the more time can work to your advantage.

It's only human to focus on the here and now. We sometimes make assumptions that affect how we plan, or fail to plan. We work hard for our money and we are tempted to live for today by rewarding ourselves with a new home or luxury car, and thinking we have plenty of time.

You can't measure time in days the way you can money in dollars because every day is different.

Jorge Luis Borges

You and your family deserve a secure financial future long after those rewards are gone.

The advantage of youth is that we have a lot of time, so the amount of money we need to target toward retirement will be small. As we get older, our strategies will change, and the amount of money will change because our time frame becomes shorter.

Time is everything. Anything you want, anything you accomplish–pleasure, success, fortune–is measured in time.

Joyce C. Hall

Getting An Early Start Is A Smart Move

	Early Bird*	Late Bloomer*
Began Investing	36 years old	46 years old
Annual Investment	$4,000	$4,000
Total Investment	$80,000	$80,000
Avg. Rate of Return	10%	10%
Stopped Investing	55 Years Old	65 Years Old
Nest Egg at 65	$653,649	$252,020

These hypothetical examples are not intended to show the performance of any investment, for any period of time, or fluctuations in principal value or investment return. Periodic investment plans do not assure a profit or protect against loss in declining markets.

As illustrated above, let's say you start your investment strategies for retirement at age 36, and add to your investment each year until age 55. Then you stop making contributions and simply let your residual investment grow for the ten years remaining until retirement.

You would be much better off than if you waited ten years to invest (at age 46), and stopped investing at age 65, even though the period of contribution was the same. In fact, at an equal rate of return, you would need to invest up to three times as much just to accumulate the same amount of money for your retirement.

Already in the retirement race?
Maybe you should pick up the pace.

If you've already started investing for retirement, then you've taken an important step in the right direction

---

*Nothing would be done at all if we waited
until it could be done so well that no one
could find fault with it.*

Cardinal Newman

But the question is whether the steps you've taken are big enough to produce the kind of results you'll need at 65.

For example, some people feel more comfortable putting their retirement savings in low-risk, low-yielding investments because they don't want to take any chances with it. The simple fact is that if you put $1,000 in a 3 percent money market account, when you retire in 20 years, that account value will only pay for one month of expenses. Pretty scary isn't it?

But if you have a broad time horizon, as people often do with their retirement investments, you can generally weather a higher level of risk than you might think.

By investing more aggressively, you'll take on a greater degree of risk, but you will also have greater potential to build your investment over time. Aggressive investments tend to be more sensitive to downward volatility in the stock and bond markets. However, remember that by determining your time frame, the longer you hold your investment, the easier it is to ride out the market's ups and downs.

So, when you know the length of time you have for retirement and it's far off, you may want to consider investments that offer greater return potential.

Every day puts you one step closer.
Don't let retirement sneak up on you.

Remember that doing *something* is always better than doing nothing. As we educate ourselves, we can then make the adjustments needed to reap the most out of our investments.

✎ **Activity**

....

- Determine the age at which you want to retire.

- How long between today and the day you retire?

- Check the options you have available to save for retirement.

- Based on your options, determine which options are for short-, medium-, and long-term time frames.

- Calculate your retirement needs.

- Choose a portfolio based on your goals and time frame.

- Determine the risk/reward ratio.

10 Factor

Age

*Where are you going? And what
are you doing to get there?*
Author Unknown

Factor

Age

Weight

As you know, age plays an important part in any weight loss program. We all know that managing your weight is hard work. The very idea of beginning a new reducing program is enough to depress anyone and set him or her off on an eating spree.

Sometimes it may seem easier to lose weight as you get older if you have always been heavy. That may sound absurd, but those who struggle with their weight most of their lives have already developed some of the strategies from the experience of constantly fighting the battle. For example, there are those, like me, who have done the yo-yo diet thing and have always had a problem maintaining weight and fitness.

However, some people are fortunate enough to maintain a fairly consistent weight and body size most of their lives. When these people finally reach an age when the body's processes begin changing and their weight and body size change, they often find it difficult to switch weight management strategies because it is a new experience. I have always had to watch what I eat. I have "dieted" many times and discovered that by applying the same factors I used for wealth management to weight management, I achieved success.

Just remember that no matter how long you've been under-fit or over-fat, no matter how old you are, it is never to late to manage your weight. This isn't a new diet (we already know there is no such thing as a "diet"); it's the beginning of a new life. Taking responsibility for your life, regardless of your age, can be quite a turn on. Finding new methods for achieving this will give you a great sense of accomplishment.

Wherever you are, be there.
Emerson

We talked about the time factor and how important time is to the success of your weight and wealth program. When you are deciding what program will best suit your situation, you will need to consult your doctor, especially if you've decided that you may need diet aids and controls as weapons in the struggle.

Without labor, nothing prospers.
Sophocles

Just as not every reducing idea will appeal to everyone, variation of those concepts will depend on your age. Something that will be effective at a young age will not necessarily work in middle age or when you're older.

The deep satisfaction that success will bring can carry you through the different stages of your life.

The beginning is the most important part of the work.

Plato

There are certain facts to keep in mind that are helpful in planning a weight loss program for your particular age. You have probably noticed that it was easier to lose weight when you were younger. There are many reasons for this, but one is that people under 30 generally have more fat free mass, and fat free mass uses more calories that fat mass. In addition, the average person will lose 7-9 pounds of muscle mass every decade past the age of 20 due to the natural aging process.

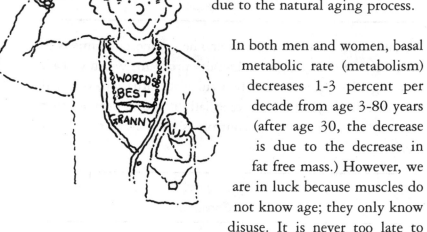

In both men and women, basal metabolic rate (metabolism) decreases 1-3 percent per decade from age 3-80 years (after age 30, the decrease is due to the decrease in fat free mass.) However, we are in luck because muscles do not know age; they only know disuse. It is never too late to build muscle mass. In fact, the only way to counteract the natural aging process of muscle loss is to begin a strength-training program.

> *Action, to be effective, must be directed*
> *to clearly conceived ends.*
> > *J. Nehru*

In What Stage of Weight Management Are You?

20-30 Years

Objectives often involve major, long-term lifestyle goals:
- *Improving eating habits: eating balanced meals with little or no fast food, minimizing alcohol*
- *Developing a pattern for fitness for life: making exercise a priority*

During this time period, the individual may be starting a new job, a new family, or living alone for the first time. It is necessary to realize the importance of eating well-balanced, nutritious meals. This time will set the stage for the rest of your life. If you develop good habits now, it will be easier to control your weight in later years.

> *Look to today. Procrastination is the art*
> *of keeping up with yesterday.*
> > *Don Marquis*

40-Something

Objectives often involve improving the quality of the present, while keeping the future in mind:
- *Increasing activity to counteract decline in fat free mass*
- *Re-evaluating the exercise program and your eating habits*
- *Increasing resistance (weight) training*

- *Instilling good habits in your children*
- *Monitoring your aging parents*
- *Planning activities and dining habits to remain within the goals already established as you may have more leisure time and opportunities to dine out*
- *Cultivating good relationships with your physicians*

As you get closer to retirement and becoming an "empty nester," you will need to re-evaluate your goals and eating/exercise programs to make sure that you are "staying the course" and not straying from your plan. It is easier to dine out and you may have more leisure time. You must make sure that you are investing the correct proportion of exercise to match your eating habits.

Age is not important unless you're a cheese.
Helen Hayes

50-Something

Objectives focus on current lifestyle improvements and longevity:

- *Re-evaluating life style and adjusting your eating and exercise habits accordingly to minimize injuries*
- *Understanding the changes of menopause for women and how that relates to spouse, significant other, and/or children*
- *Continuing annual physical check-ups*

Keep in mind that as you continue to age, you need to continue resistance training and aerobic activity to maintain fitness levels. You are undergoing physical changes that can affect your ability to metabolize your food and lose weight.

Osteoporosis is more of a concern for women, and early detection of any disease is the key to longevity.

You only live once, but if you work it right,
once is enough.

Joe E. Lewis

---

60 +

Objectives involve protecting a healthy lifestyle and remaining fit in both mind and body:
- *Maximizing nutritious meals that are not too "filling"*
- *Continuing preventative medicine*
- *Continuing aerobic and resistance exercise*

Studies have shown that those who remain active both physically and mentally remain "younger" than their counterparts who do not. The key to health, fitness, and controlled weight in the "golden years" is to remain as active in both mind and body as possible. Don't be hesitant to try new activities, be it painting or water aerobics.

I never feel age...If you have creative work,
you don't have age or time.

Louise Nevelson

---

*Before beginning any weight loss and exercise plan, an individual should consult with his or her doctor.

✎ Activity

··

- Determine at what stage of life you are.

- Use your journal to do a checklist of your priorities.

- Review your goals and objectives.

- Make the necessary changes to move forward.

If I had known I was going to live this long, I would have planned better.

Edward B. Heller

Factor 10

Age

Wealth

My father passed away August 19, 1998, at age 89. He had a lot of illnesses in his lifetime. At age 48, he had throat cancer; a brain tumor at age 62; his gallbladder removed at age 80; and at age 84, bypass surgery on his right leg. He didn't think he would live to retirement, let alone 24 years longer! Because he didn't feel he would live long, *"he did not plan to fail, he failed to plan!"*

Age is always an important investment consideration because it creates a natural time horizon for your investment program. The good news is we could live a long time. Death is not necessarily the horizon we are planning for. Retirement is clearly the time when your income usually declines. Therefore, you invest to make up for the shortfall.

Because we have no way of knowing how long we will live, we need to plan for every stage of our lives. In general, the younger you are, the more risk you can afford to take because your longer investment horizon will provide the time it takes to make up for investment losses. But remember, that doesn't mean that if you are starting when you are older or retired, you should invest too conservatively. (You will always need to invest a percent of your portfolio for growth.)

The keys to planning your savings are how close you are to retirement and the level of investment risk you're comfortable with. Even people in their 60s and 70s need to invest for growth as well as income, because they will still live long enough to be affected by inflation.

Consider your potential life expectancy:

Present Age	Life Expectancy
30	52.2
35	47.3
40	42.5
45	37.7
50	33.1
55	28.6
60	24.2
65	20.0
70	16.0

Your stage of life will determine what investment strategies you will use.

Who can say with certainty that one will live to see tomorrow?

Tibetan proverb

What Stage Investor Are You?

Early Stage*
Objectives often involve major, long-term lifestyle goals:
- *Improving lifestyle*
- *Saving for a home or other major purchases*
- *Starting a family and educating children*
- *Beginning a sound retirement program*

Investor Profile: Early Years—20s and 30s**

Conservative
- 40% ....Growth & Income
- 30% ....Income
- 20% ....Balanced
- 10% ....Global Growth

Moderate
- 35% ....Growth & Income
- 25% ....Growth
- 20% ....Global Growth
- 20% ....Income

Aggressive
- 45% ....Growth
- 30% ....Global Growth
- 15% ....Growth & Income
- 10% ....Income

Do what you can where you are with what you've got.

Theodore Roosevelt

Mid Career*

Goals often involve improving the quality of the present, without jeopardizing the future:

- *Increasing current income to pay tuition cost*
- *Enhancing income to fund the care of a parent*
- *Financing more recreational activities or long vacations*
- *Purchasing a major discretionary item (boat, second car, camper)*

Investor Profile: Middle Years—40s**

Conservative

40%	Income
30%	Growth & Income
20%	Balanced
10%	Global Growth

Moderate

35%	Income
25%	Growth & Income
20%	Balanced
20%	Global Growth

Aggressive

30%	Global Growth
30%	Growth
20%	Growth & Income
20%	Income

Life is a no deposit, no return endeavor.
Author Unknown

Peak Earnings*

Goals focus on major current lifestyle improvements and long-term security:

- *Minimizing taxes*
- *Taking early retirement*
- *Increasing leisure activities and travel time*
- *Building a second home or future retirement home*
- *Helping out parents, children, and grandchildren*
- *Increasing wealth and building an estate to pass to heirs*

Investor Profile: Maturing Years–50s**

Conservative

60%	Income
20%	Growth & Income
15%	Balanced
5%	Global Growth

Moderate

50%	Income
25%	Growth & Income
15%	Balanced
10%	Global Growth

Aggressive

40%	Income
25%	Growth & Income
20%	Growth
15%	Global Growth

---

*Life is lived in the present. Yesterday has
gone, tomorrow is yet to be. Today is the miracle.*
Author Unknown

Spending it all
A couple bought an expensive motor home and traveled from state to state leisurely seeing the sights. They wrote their friend a letter that began: "Having such a great time, we decided to retire and enjoy spending our children's inheritance."

Retirement*
Goals involve protecting a desirable lifestyle and building a legacy:
- *Maximizing income to meet living expenses*
- *Keeping pace with inflation and protecting purchasing power*
- *Paying for special trips and leisure purchases*
- *Preserving funds for unexpected medical costs*
- *Helping out children and funding college for grandchildren*

Investor Profile: Retirement Years–60s +**

Conservative

70%	Income
15%	Balanced
10%	Growth & Income
5%	Global Growth

Moderate

60%	Income
20%	Growth & Income
10%	Balanced
10%	Global Growth

Aggressive

50%	Income
20%	Growth & Income
15%	Growth
15%	Global Growth

*Before investing, an individual should have the equivalent of 3-6 months of expenses in a money market account for a cash reserve.

**These sample portfolios are not intended as investment advice. However you can—with the help of an investment advisor—diversify your portfolio with different types of investment products.

✎ Activity

....

- Determine at what stage of life you are.

- Use your journal to do a checklist of your priorities.

- Review your goals and objectives.

- Make the necessary changes to move forward.

Factor 11

Needs vs. Wants

> *Your dreams can be realities. They are the stuff that leads us through life toward great happiness.*
>
> Deborah Norville

Factor 11

Needs vs. Wants

Weight

The travel agent told this story...

A man called, furious about a Florida vacation package we did. I asked him what was wrong with the vacation in Orlando. He said he needed, wanted, and was expecting an ocean-view room. I tried to explain that is not possible, since Orlando is in the middle of the state. He replied, "Don't lie to me. I looked on the map and Florida is a very thin state."

Are you in the habit of asking yourself whether you need or want a food item before you eat it? That brings up a very important point. We learned of the influence our parents had on the way we manage our weight when discussing the family factor. Now it is time to use that information to educate yourself on the **needs** and **wants** of weight management. Sometimes you will find that it is necessary to turn the wants into needs, and the needs into wants! If you eat what you

want, you may find that you physically are not what you **need** to be! If you eat what you **need,** you may find that you physically become what you **want** to be!

Dig where the gold is, unless you just need some exercise.

John M. Capozzi

If we think that food will make us happy, we might be inclined to spend our food calories on things we don't need because we feel it will make us happy. The truth is, we **need** to control our food intake and manage our weight to have the health and long-term weight management we desire. We **want** to use good weight management to fulfill the need for good health.

By letting ourselves know what we need, we simply give ourselves a complete picture with which to make good decisions. If we are not honest with ourselves, it can be destructive and lead to poor choices that we will regret later.

Sometimes it's better to ask ourselves what we don't want:

- We don't want to have serious health problems.
- We don't want to fight with others or ourselves about weight management.
- We don't want to disappoint the people who depend on us.
- We don't want to deny ourselves what we enjoy eating.
- We don't want to engage in "yo-yo" dieting.
- We don't want to be unfit and never exercise.

Once we figure out what we do not want, it's easier to understand what we do want. Then we can see the difference between needs and wants.

I don't live to eat; I eat to live.
                                        Edward B. Heller

Are you eating because you need to eat or because you want to eat? Some people live to eat. Are you eating because you think it will make you happy? When you decide to eat a certain food item, are you choosing to eat it because it is nutritious, or because you think it will taste good? There is nothing wrong with eating things that taste good. Really, would you choose to eat something that tastes awful? What you must keep in mind is the ratio of calories to fat, and whether or not you want to spend those calories on that particular food item. In other words, do I **need** to eat this, or do I **want** to eat this. You may really **want** to eat that hot fudge sundae, but you already have eaten several cookies that day, so should you eat that sundae just because you want it? Maybe you should set a goal and eat less fat the next day so you can eat that hot fudge sundae!

Explore alternatives that will keep you from impulse eating. Use your journal to write down everything you eat. Keep track of the calories and fat grams. Then you will know if you can afford to eat something just because you want it, not just because you need it. It is important to realize on a good weight management program, you do not deny yourself everything you want! Sometimes you may feel you **need** that item you **want!**

That is why it is called management and not a diet. On a diet, you can only eat certain foods. In good weight management, you decide how you can eat the things you enjoy, while still having healthy, nutritious eating habits.

The best climber in the world is the one who is having the most fun.
Alex Lowe

Let's not forget exercise. You may know that you should exercise, and that you need to exercise, but do you want to exercise? How can we help change that need to a want?

- Exercise with a friend or buddy. It is always easier to share an activity!

- Explore your options and choose the things you like to do (walking, jogging, group exercise, biking, hiking, spinning, climbing, resistance training, gardening, rowing, skiing, skating, etc.) The exercise possibilities are endless.

- Vary the exercise. Cross training is important! Do different exercises on different days.

I generally avoid temptation unless I can't resist it.
Mae West

What mental picture do you have when thinking about how you want to look? We discussed visualizing and your attitude regarding your weight management. When it comes to how you want to look, explore these factors; it will help when making the final decision about what you will and will not eat.

Think about the consequences of over-indulging yourself.

You become:
Unfit
Unhappy
Overweight
Out-of-shape
Guilty
Weak minded
Embarrassed

Also think about the consequences of under-indulging yourself.

You become:
Tense
Depressed
Resentful
Nervous
Deprived (Never satisfied)
Angry
Jealous

It is our choices that show what we truly are, far more than our abilities.
J.K.Rowling

As you can see, too much of a good thing can be as bad as too little of a good thing. You have to find that happy medium; that place where you can control what you eat, and eat what you need as well as what you want. There is nothing wrong with eating things you want. A good weight management program will allow you to eat those things that you want, as long as you eat those things in moderation. Balance your needs and wants. Plan for those days when you know you will go to a party. More importantly, remember that it is okay if you do not follow your weight management plan to the letter everyday. There will be times when you have to eat something you want...that's okay! Don't be so hard on yourself when that happens. Just make sure it is the exception, not the rule.

✎ Activity

- Every morning for the next week write down the food and exercise you need. Then write down things you want. Compare the two: circle the items in both columns that are the same.

- Evaluate the items that are the same; be honest with yourself. Do you really need to eat that food item and do that exercise? If you do, put a star next to it.

- Review your food budget and decide how you will "pay" for the item. Do you have to exercise more, eat fewer calories, or is it already on your food budget? Can you work the exercise into your schedule?

- Do this process with each of the circled items.

- Don't eat the food item right away. Determine if you have changed your mind about needing or wanting that item.

- Decide if the exercise will help you "diversify your exercise portfolio." If so, can you work it into your schedule?

- Think about what is going on in your life right now that might be affecting your eating and exercising decisions.

> *Don't always follow the crowd, because nobody goes there anymore.*
>
> *Yogi Berra*

Factor

Needs vs. Wants

Wealth

Are you in the habit of asking yourself whether you **need** or **want** an item before you purchase it? That brings up a very important point. When we evaluated ourselves in the family factor, we realized what impact our parents had on the way we treat money. This is where you use that information to educate yourself on the **needs**, not **wants**, of buying.

> *Grasp the opportunity to manage change, not avoid it.*
>
> *Author Unknown*

If we think that spending money will make us happy, we might be inclined to spend our money on things we don't need because we feel it will make us happy. The truth is we need to live below our means to have the financial security we desire.

By letting ourselves know what we **need**, we simply give ourselves a complete picture with which to make good decisions. If we are not honest with ourselves, it can be destructive financially.

Sometimes it's better to ask ourselves what we don't want:

- We don't want to have serious financial problems.

- We don't want to fight with others about money.

- We don't want to deny ourselves a secure financial retirement.

- We don't want to live hand to mouth.

- We don't want to disappoint the people who depend on us.

- We don't want to make investment mistakes.

Once we figure out what we *don't* want, it's easier to understand what we *do* want. Then we can see the difference between needs and wants.

Do you find it easy to tell yourself no? You read this to some extent in Factor Four–Habits. Before you spend money, ask yourself if you really **want** to spend the money. For example, put the item in the cart at the department store and walk around; think about your choices. If you really **need** to buy the item go ahead, but if you only **want** the item, put it back. If you have difficulty making good decisions, you might use the buddy system and take a friend with you when you are shopping to keep from making bad choices.

Explore alternatives to shopping that will keep you from impulse buying.

Seek not outside yourself, success is within.
Mary Lou Cook

What mental picture do you have when thinking about your financial future? We discussed visualizing and your attitude toward your finances. When it comes to wealth, explore these factors; it will help when making the final decision to buy.

Think about the consequences of over-indulging yourself.

You become: *Bored*
                     Ungrateful
                     Unhappy
                     Belligerent
                     Obnoxious
                     Guilty
                     Weak minded
                     Embarrassed

Also think about the consequences of under-indulging yourself.

You become: *Tense*
                     Depressed
                     Resentful
                     Nervous
                     Deprived (Never satisfied)
                     Angry
                     Jealous

As you can see, too much of a good thing can be as bad as not enough of a good thing.

✎ Activity

· ·

- Every morning for the next week write down things you need. Then write down things you want.

- Compare the two: circle the items in both columns that are the same.

- Evaluate the items that are the same, and be honest with yourself. Do you really need that item? If you do, put a star next to it.

- Add that item to your goals list and determine if it is a short-, intermediate, or long-term goal.

- Review your budget and decide how you will pay for the item.

- Do this process with each of the circled items.

- Don't buy the item right away. If it is on your short-term list, wait a week, and determine after that time if you have changed your mind about needing or wanting that item.

- When thinking about the circled items, ask yourself what emotion is prompting your need. Remember your attitude factors; go back and review that factor.

- Think about what is going on in your life right now that might be affecting your buying decisions.

Factor **12**

Risk

Factor

Risk

Weight

A hungry lion was roaming through the jungle looking for something to eat. He came across two men. One was sitting under a tree reading a book; the other typing away on his typewriter. The lion quickly pounced on the man reading the book and devoured him. Even the king of the jungle knows that readers digest, and writers cramp.

Now that you have stopped groaning, you might think that the lion "weighed" his risk and made an appropriate choice. Risk in weight management is very real, and it is all about choices. Many people try to lose weight too quickly and in an unsafe manner without seeking medical help. Before initiating any weight management program, you should ALWAYS seek the advice of your doctor. There are many products that claim "miracle" weight loss, but many of these are actually harmful to the body.

Americans today feel that being thin at any price is worth the risk, and try fad diets for quick weight loss. These can be damaging to health by losing too much too fast. It is that unrealistic outlook that affects our health and our future.

There are new "diets" on the market everyday. Most recently the high protein diets have come to the forefront. You probably know at least a dozen people who have tried or are on one! We have previously discussed why many of the high protein diets are difficult to use for maintaining long-term weight management. Other diets that are nutritionally inadequate can actually cause health problems, and some diets are boring because you eat the same food repeatedly, or are difficult to continue.

"Diets" work, but only as a short-term solution

The two most important things to remember when starting any weight management program are: one, to consult your physician and two, there is no such thing as a "diet." You must make a decision to eat this way for the rest of your life. Anything else results in yo-yo dieting. Many people will go on a safe weight loss program and lose weight. When the goal is reached, they fail to maintain correct eating and exercise habits and gain back all the weight originally lost, sometimes even more!

Be not afraid of growing slowly; be afraid of standing still.

Chinese proverb

Risk in weight management comes in many forms. There is the risk of fad diets, falling off a weight loss program when you are tempted by your favorite foods or reach a plateau, not re-evaluating your goals and objectives, or feeling deprived when others are eating and you can't. Anything worthwhile has some risk, but through informed, sensible decisions, you can minimize the risk.

It is important to educate, determine goals, evaluate motivation, decide on a timeframe, and look at age so we can make the best decisions regarding our weight management program.

Life is like a bicycle. You don't fall off unless you stop pedaling.
                                        Unknown

Sometimes there is more to risk than meets the eye. Risk in weight management is a creature of many faces. When we take too much risk, our expectations are a higher rate of return for our investments than is realistic. We expect to lose a lot of weight, do it quickly, and keep it off; this rarely happens. In other words, investing in "quick" weight loss strategies might actually sabotage our goals. If we look to others for answers, rather than fully understanding our choices, we will be unsuccessful and actually "lose" our investment (our sense of self-worth and/or our health) instead of the weight.

If you fell down yesterday, stand up today.
                                        H.G. Wells

So, what is the correlation between dieting and weight loss? How much weight loss is lean body mass as opposed to fat mass? This is a factor to be explored when determining the risk associated with weight loss. As previously stated, the goal is to reduce fat mass and increase lean body mass. If too much weight is lost too quickly, then lean body mass is also lost.

It has been determined that diet and exercise are the "dynamic duo" for weight loss. In an article published by the *International Journal of Obesity*, 436 studies over the past 25 years were analyzed. Exercise alone was the least effective means of weight loss, reduction of percent body fat, and increase of basal metabolism. Weight loss through diet alone, and diet and exercise showed about the same amount of weight loss. However, diet and exercise together tended to be the superior program over time. In addition, with diet and exercise combined, the risk of losing lean muscle mass was also reduced, because those who used diet alone to reduce weight lost 25 percent muscle, but those who used diet and exercise combined lost a small amount of muscle and more fat mass.

What does this mean? This could be interpreted to mean that the risk of failure is less with diet and exercise, as it becomes a lifestyle change rather than just a "diet." Again, one must look at the weight loss program as a permanent change in lifestyle, not a temporary "diet."

How much to invest in a particular "diet" depends on your tolerance for risk, your health goals, time frame, age, etc.

A good beginning is half the battle.
Portuguese proverb

Let's take a look at some of the various risk factors for weight loss.

1. Fad Diets

As mentioned before, these diets usually make unrealistic weight loss claims. Many are unproven, claim to "melt" fat away, or assert that there is no need to exercise. Usually if a "diet" seems too good to be true, it is. Also, many fad diets are unhealthy because these diets do not provide proper nutrition, and more muscle mass, not fat mass occurs in the weight loss due to too rapid a loss.

Fat-Free Diet   Fasting Diet

Protein Diet

2. Diet Programs

There are many safe and proven diet programs on the market. These programs often have dieticians, nutritionists, and physicians affiliated with the pro-

Grapefruit Diet   Cabbage Soup Diet

Low-Carb Diet   Lo-Cal Diet

gram. Many of these programs are safe and effective for weight management. So what could be risky about that? These programs are costly and require you to eat their food. If you stay with the program and follow their maintenance schedule, you will lose weight and keep it off. If you leave the program and go back to your old habits, the weight will return and you will have lost your investment.

3. Exercise Injuries

While it is true that diet and exercise are an integral part of an exercise program, the risk of injury from improper exercise looms large. Before you start on an exercise program, check with your doctor. Get the help of a personal trainer or exercise specialist. Don't decide that you can go out and run three miles if you have not been exercising. Start slowly by walking for 10-20 minutes, then increase the duration. The same is true for resistance exercise. Start with low weight and build up to heavier weight. In addition, cross train and change the form of exercise every few weeks. After all, variety is the spice of life! Make sure you don't overdo it and risk injury before you even get started!

4. Joining a Health Club

Joining a health club can be expensive, so be sure you will stick to the program before you make that financial investment. Find a health club that has a trial membership, or a month-to-month membership. Talk to your friends and neighbors to find out if the club has a good reputation. Call the Better Business Bureau and investigate the club, or go online and search for information.

5. Using Home Exercise Videos

Many people prefer to exercise at home and for various reasons. Some feel they are too overweight or clumsy to be seen in public;

others like to exercise alone. Whatever the reasons for exercising at home and using videos, make sure that the video is safe and effective. Check reviews for home exercise videos; ask your friends and neighbors about the ones they may use. You can borrow them or rent them from your library or video store, so it is a cost-effective method, but there are inherent dangers to exercising alone (injury, over-exertion, etc.).

6. Diet aids

There are many drugs to aid in your battle of the bulge. Some of them are over-the-counter (OTC) drugs; some of them are prescription drugs. Many of the over-the-counter drugs contain ingredients that could react with other medications you may be taking, cause an allergic reaction, etc., so be sure to check the ingredient label before you use any over-the-counter drug. In addition to OTC drugs, there are prescription drugs to assist in weight management. Talk with your doctor to see if you meet the criteria to use these drugs. As with any drug, be sure that you follow the directions and use it safely.

It is not enough to get things done; they must be done right.

Arthur T. Hadley

Once you find a weight management program that is good for you and with which you can live, stick to your decision. Don't fall into the pattern of yo-yo dieting. Find a safe program that combines healthy eating, safe exercise, and a cost you can afford to minimize your risk.

Remember to:

- *Assess your risks.*

Research the weight management program you are about to begin. Make sure it is safe and effective and a program that you can "stick" with for the long term. Check with your doctor.

- *Know your investment.*

Educate yourself, weigh the pros and cons of your weight management program, reevaluate your goals and objectives every 4-6 months, and adjust your eating and exercise habits as your time frame and goals change.

- *Don't try to lose too much too fast.*

Weight loss that occurs too quickly (more than 1.6 pounds per week) is not just loss of fat mass, but loss of lean body mass as well. Lean body mass burns more calories than fat mass, so don't reduce your investment by over-reducing too quickly.

- *Cross train when exercising.*

Don't get stuck in a rut and end up being bored with your exercise program. Do aerobic training as well as resistance training, and change the order or type of exercise every few weeks.

- *Keep a long-term perspective.*

You did not gain the weight you are trying to lose overnight. Be patient and give yourself time to lose the weight slowly and safely; make it a lifestyle change that you can keep for the rest of your life.

✎ Activity

....

Ask yourself these questions:

- Have I consulted a physician before starting on my weight loss program?

  Always consult your physician before starting any weight loss program to insure that the program is safe for you. Health screening is a priority.

- How much weight do I realistically expect to lose?

  Am I 10, 20, 30, or more pounds overweight?
  Consider a conservative mixture of diet and exercise to achieve first short-term goals and then expand to long-term, lifetime goals.

- Do I expect to lose the weight quickly, or am I realistic about the time frame?

  Rapid weight loss results in loss of lean body mass as well as fat mass. Be patient and lose weight at a rate of no more than 1.6 pounds a week.

- Do I plan on joining a weight loss program or health club?

  Consider the cost of these programs and your ability to stay committed for the long term. Some people need this kind of support, just make sure it is right for you.

- When starting an exercise program, will it be safe and effective for me?

  Remember to check with your physician, vary the workout and don't overdo. You want to continue this for a long time...the rest of your life.

To conquer without risk is to triumph without glory.

El Cid

Risk

Wealth

Progress involves risk—you can't steal second and keep your foot on first.
Speed Queen News

Is risk really what we think it is? The amount of risk tolerance varies from person to person, but the lack of knowledge and understanding of what risk really is can cost you where it hurts the most—your quality of life.

Americans today feel that if they're careful with their money, they can live their lives without risk. It's that unrealistic outlook that affects our financial lives.

As interest rates fall to their lowest levels in the last decade, those that played it safe with certificates of deposit, treasury bills and other "risk-free" investments are feeling the pain.

Risk comes in many guises. There is the risk of doing something, in being either too aggressive or too conservative. Additionally, there is the risk that times will change, and you won't. You can't avoid some risk in investing, but through informed, sensible decisions, you can control it.

We must educate ourselves, determine our goals, evaluate our motivation, figure our time, and consider our age so we can invest our money in the best manner available to us. Taking an informed risk is better than trying to avoid all risk by doing nothing.

Sometimes there's more to risk than meets the eye. And sometimes what looks like risk is really an opportunity for growth. Risk is a creature of many faces, and when we take risks, our expectations are for a higher rate of return on our investments. (I know it sounds scary, but risk really does equal reward!)

---

*There would be nothing to frighten you
if you refused to be afraid.*

Gandhi

One of the major problems is how to define risk. Risk is almost always used as a synonym for volatility. For investors, there is an enormous difference between risk and volatility in the real world of consequences.

The same investment could be low-risk or high-risk, depending on the time frame. It would be low-risk if it's meant to finance a child's college education fifteen years away, but high-risk if it represents the down payment to be made on a house in six months. Because risk ratings are typically given for periods of a year or less, investors might be using short-term evaluations to construct long-term portfolios.

We also need to question the accuracy of the correlation (paralleled or reciprocal relationship) established between different asset classes. When we look at all the facts and figures, is it possible to determine what the correlation is going to be over the next 10-20 years? It is a fantasy to think we can figure out what the correlation is likely to be between small companies and mid-sized companies, and real estate and international portfolios.

How much you want to invest in a particular asset class depends on your tolerance for risk, your tax situation goals, time frame, age, etc.

Let's take a look at the various types of risk:

1. Market Risk
This is the risk most people think of when they think of risk. They are afraid that the entire market will fall and take even the best stocks with it. If market risk is a concern, you can minimize your risk by diversifying your portfolio (not putting all of your eggs in one basket).

You can diversify three ways:

- *Diversify among various investment alternatives. (stocks, mutual funds, bonds)*
- *Diversify within a particular type of investment by investing in several different companies (all utility, health care, transportation companies).*

- *Diversify in bonds or other fixed-income investments according to maturity dates.*

The best cure for the decline of an entire market is not timing the market, but time in the market. This is because over time, the stock market inevitably goes up.

You can also reduce the risk of buying shares at the top of the cycle with a simple strategy called dollar-cost averaging, which means buying fixed dollar amounts of shares at regular intervals. This strategy works because when prices are the highest, you buy the fewest shares, and vice versa.

When owning a stock, there is also the possibility that the stock will stumble, or that its industry will go into a decline. The antidote to this ill is to spread your money across a broad assortment of stocks. This is where mutual funds shine.

What is a mutual fund?

A mutual fund pools capital (money) and makes investments on your behalf. A professional money manager invests the fund's asset in many securities. The share price of the portfolio is determined at the close of each business day. The shareholders of a mutual fund are its owners, and they are entitled to all of the fund's net income and gains. Investors can select from a variety of mutual funds. There are more than 10,000 different mutual fund companies. (The good news is you don't have to learn about all of them.) Any capital gains and dividends received from these mutual funds must be claimed as ordinary income the year they are received. Proper timing and consistent investments over a prolonged period of time also protect against market risk.

> *By carefully balancing portfolio risks,*
> *you can make them work in your favor.*

2. Default Risk

Default risk is the chance that a corporation or unit of government will be unable to make payments of interest and principal on its debt. Debt instruments are referred to as bonds. Your best shield against default is a high safety rating from the rating agencies.

There are two rating agencies for bonds: Moody's and Standard & Poor's (S&P).

Investment grade bonds (those rated BBB or higher by Standard & Poor's or Baa or higher by Moody's Investors Service) have an almost infinitesimal default rate. On the other hand, almost 1 out of 20 junk-bond issuers (rated BB or below by S&P, BA or below by Moody's) default in any given year, says Moody's. Some investments carry guarantees of repayment; either directly (U.S. Treasury debt), indirectly (mortgage-based securities issued by U. S. government agencies), or by contract (municipal bonds insured by private companies). Don't despair: your investment advisor will help you make these investment decisions. If you don't currently have an investment advisor ask a friend for a referral.

3. Interest-Rate Risk

Interest rate risk, or money rate risk, is the risk of change in the price of a fixed-income security resulting from a change in the interest paid on securities currently being issued. When interest rates rise, the market prices of previously issued bonds tend to decline. When interest rates fall, the prices of previously issued bonds tend to rise.

Example: You buy a $1,000 bond that yields 8 percent. Then prevailing interest rates for similar bonds rise to 9 percent. Your bond is instantly worthless should you try to sell it because buyers won't pay $1,000 for an 8 percent bond when they can get a similar bond at 9 percent. How badly your bond will be battered by an increase in rates depends on the time remaining until it matures. The shorter the time, the less sensitive the price is to changes in interest rates. Here's how that market value of a bond yielding 8 percent would be affected by increases in interest rates of one and two percentage points:

Years to maturity of bond	Loss of Market Value if:	
	Rates rise one point	Rates rise two points
2.5	-2%	-4%
10	-7	-13
30	-10	-19

To reduce interest-rate risk, keep maturities of bonds you own to several years or shorter, or buy short-term bond funds which usually have average weighted maturities three years or less. Oddly enough, junk bonds are hurt less by higher interest rates because their yields are already abnormally high.

You can reduce interest-rate risk by buying short-term bonds or bond funds.

4. Reinvestment Risk

Four years ago, perhaps you put your money away in a great 8 percent certificate of deposit (CD). That CD has now matured, and you must reinvest the proceeds at a time when three-year CDs yield a pitiful 4 percent. Or your 9 percent municipal bond, bought 10 years ago, is called (retired early), and you face a municipal bond market giving 6 percent yields on similar bonds. Or the twice-yearly income from your 10 percent treasury bond must be reinvested at today's 7 percent treasury yields.

A way around this dark alley is to ladder the maturities of CDs or bonds-invest equal amounts in issues maturing in, say, one through five years in the case of CDs or two through ten years for bonds. Today, with interest rates unusually low, laddering maturities of bonds also protect you against the hazard of higher interest rates.

If rates do rise, some of your holdings can be reinvested relatively soon.

5. Inflation Risk

Two old-timers were discussing a mutual friend. Said one, "Poor old John seems to be living in the past." "And why not?" replied the other. "It's a lot cheaper."

Inflation risk is the decrease in your portfolio's value due to the reduction of your money's purchasing power. If you have an inflation factor of 3.5 percent, the dollar you spend today will need to be doubled in twenty years to spend the same. If the inflation factor is 4.5 percent, the dollar you spend today will need to be doubled in fifteen years to spend the same.

If the return on your savings doesn't keep up with inflation, your savings will not grow as you had planned, and you may reach retirement without enough income (or spending power) to live as comfortably as you might like. People who take little investment risk—investing only in what they consider to be "safe investments"—may earn a lower rate of return and expose their savings to higher inflation risk. For example, if your investments returned 8 percent over a certain period, but inflation rate was 3 percent, then your real return would be 5 percent. When choosing investments, it is important to consider inflation's effect on the rate of return you hope to achieve.

6. *Liquidity Risk*

Liquidity risk is the improper allocation of investments into areas not meant for short-term investments. Penalties of loss of principal can occur when funds are liquidated. It's a snap to sell blue-chip stocks. But in a pinch, try unloading a limited partnership or a big position in an obscure over-the-counter stock. A hasty, forced sale could mean a significant loss. The solution is obvious: avoid limited partnerships and stick to stocks and mutual funds that are widely traded. And, of course, the proper investments for the proper time frame are crucial.

Duck excessive volatility with a portfolio of stocks, bonds and T-bills.

Ways to measure risk:

Standard Deviation:

This is a single, known statistic. This term is a proxy for total risk-free return of a three-month treasury bill. Measure the extent to which a fund, stock, or bond exceeds that rate of return. Call this the excess return. Standard deviation is a measure of how reliable that rate of excess return is from week to week (or month to month) over, say, two or three years. This gives you an indication of how much volatility to expect from an investment. The greater that volatility, the higher the standard deviation, hence the risk, of an investment. Understandably, investments with high rates of return also carry high standard deviations.

---

*We each build our own future. We are
the architects of our own fortune.*
                                    Appius Caecus

Example Standard Deviations

Aggressive-growth funds	5.29
International funds	4.60
Long-term-growth funds	4.45
Growth and Income funds	3.84
S&P 500 Index	4.23
High-yield corporate bond funds	2.57
Government securities funds	1.14
High quality corporate bond funds	1.12
Municipal bond funds	1.08

*How to escape market calamities: Put your money
in a variety of stocks or in mutual funds.*

Beta:

Beta measures the volatility of an investment relative to the overall market, often represented by the Standard & Poor's 500-stock index. The market always gets a beta of 1. A stock fund with a beta of 1.3 fluctuates, up or down, 30 percent more than the overall market. A fund with a beta of 0.9 fluctuates 10 percent less than the market. Since risk and reward are related, a high beta is often thought to indicate high rewards.

Beta is a measure of risk, but not a measure of expected returns.

> *University of Chicago Finance*
> *Professor Kenneth French*

Some prefer using standard deviation over beta for measuring risk when investing in stocks.

Time is the factor that will cure risk, says Carl Gargula of Ibbotson. It's crucial to understand the relationship between risk and time, and what it means to your portfolio, because time can turn risk on its ear.

Take a collection of standard investment choices: common stock, small-company stocks, long-term government bonds, intermediate government bonds and treasury bills. In any given year, which do you think would be the least risky? Chances are, you correctly picked U.S. Treasury bills, which mature in less than one year. Here, courtesy of Ibbotson, is the all-time worst performances of investments in any single year since 1926.

Worst Annual Performance

Small-company stocks	-58.0%	1937
Common stocks	-43.3%	1931
Long-term treasuries	- 9.2%	1967
Long-term corporate bonds	- 8.1%	1969
Intermediate treasuries	- 2.3%	1931
Treasury bills	- 0.1%	1938

Clearly, T-bills hurt investors least in a crunch. But over the long term, the white-knuckle bumps and jumps of small-company stocks smooth out, and collectively they become the best investments based on their likelihood of producing a good return.

The worst annualized rate of return for small-company stocks over a 20 year period was 5.7 percent (1929-48). That 20-year worst rate of annual return is better than any other class of investment.

Compare it with:

Common stocks:	3.1%	(1929-48)
Long-term corporate:	1.3%	(1950-69)
Long-term treasuries:	0.7%	(1950-69)
Intermediate treasuries:	1.6%	(1940-59)
Treasury bills:	0.4%	(1931-50)

As you would expect, nothing beats T-bills for short-term safety. In their worst year ever, they essentially broke even. But over five-, and ten-year periods, intermediate treasury bonds with average maturities of five years had the best worst-case returns. And over twenty years, volatile small-company stocks rose to the top of the heap.

Let's look at more recent data, annualized returns during 1972-91:

Annualized Returns over 20 Years

Small-company stocks	*14.6%*
Common stock	*11.9%*
Intermediate treasuries	*9.4%*
Long-term corporate bonds	*9.4%*
Long-term treasuries	*9.0%*
Treasury bills	*7.7%*

As you can see, the longer you nurture a risky investment, the greater your likelihood is of achieving a commensurate reward and the less your risk is of losing money to poor performance.

Self-trust is the essence of heroism.
Emerson

Okay... so what does all this mean? (Now that I've confused the heck out of you.) Well, as you have probably guessed, investment risk is inevitable, but how you either reduce that risk or make it work in your favor is the bottom line. Your goal should be to develop a portfolio with risks you understand and accept. A good investment advisor will help with questions.

The more experience you have with these three types of investments, the more comfortable you may be with leaving your money invested while riding out any market downturn.

Remember to:

- *Assess your risks.*

Bank CDs of $100,000 or less are government-backed and entail no default or market risk. But current CD rates certainly carry inflation and reinvestment risks.

- *Know your investment.*

Educate yourself, weigh the pros and cons of your investments, reevaluate your goals and objectives on an annual basis, and reallocate your portfolio as your time frame and goals change.

- *Don't try to time the market.*

Dollar cost averaging is a classic risk dampener. You ignore short-term market volatility by investing equal amounts on a regular basis.

- *Diversify.*

You won't suddenly strike it rich with a diversified portfolio, but you may get rich slowly and you'll sleep a whole lot better. A mutual fund is more diversified than a handful of individual stocks. Better still, invest in several funds whose managers employ different stock-picking styles.

- *Keep a long-term perspective.*

Since 1926, including the Great Depression, small-company stocks as a group have been the most lucrative investment when taken in 20-year chunks, despite their volatility. But you don't want to be a big investor in such stocks if your time frame is only a couple of years.

✎ Activity

• •

Ask yourself these questions:

- What kind of investor am I?

  Is capital preservation more important than long-term growth? If so, consider a conservative mixture of investments more heavily weighted toward bonds and short-term investments for your portfolio.

- Do I expect to withdraw or borrow 1/3 or more of this invested money within seven years?

  Under unforeseen circumstances, such as loss of income, many people need to draw on "long-term" money for short-term needs. If you don't have an emergency fund, a conservative investment approach may be the most appropriate.

- Do I have an emergency fund (savings equivalent to at least three months after-tax income)?

  The smaller the portion of total assets you're investing, the more aggressive you might wish to be in this portion of your portfolio. But even a diversified mutual fund should not be your one and only investment for your household retirement savings.

- Approximately what portion of my total investable assets is in my retirement savings plan at work?

  If your income is likely to change, you may have more or less money to meet your expenses and you may have to dip into your long-term investments. A more conservative approach may enable you to depend on money being available.

- Do I expect my earnings to increase and far outpace inflation, decrease (due to retirement, part-time work, economically depressed industry, etc.), or keep pace with inflation?

Your comfort level with investment risk is important in determining how aggressively or conservatively you choose to invest.

- When thinking about my retirement savings, where would I place myself on the following scale?

  1. I want as much assurance as possible that the value of my retirement savings will not go down.

  4. I want to maintain a balanced savings mixed with some fluctuation and growth.

  7. I want my money to grow as much as possible, regardless of risk or fluctuation.

Lowest   Highest
1 ➞ 2 ➞ 3 ➞ 4 ➞ 5 ➞ 6 ➞ 7

The more experience you have with these three types of investments, the more comfortable you may be with leaving your money invested while riding out any market downturn.

- How many dependents do I have (including spouse, children I support, elderly parents, etc.)?

- Approximately what portion of my monthly take-home income goes toward paying off debt other than a home mortgage (auto loans, credit cards, etc.)?
  Less than 10%
  Between 10% and 25%
  Between 26% and 50%
  More than 50%

If a large portion of your income goes toward paying debt, you are more likely to need cash available in case of unforeseen circumstances.

Your comfort level with investment risk is important in determining how aggressively or conservatively you choose to invest. Proper evaluation of debt plays an important role in your investment decisions.

Again, your professional advisor will help you determine your risk tolerance.

Conclusion

Some behavioral researchers say it takes 21 days of repeating a new behavior daily to create a habit. Some say 14 days, and still others say 12 months to recognize real progress. One thing for sure, it is never instant or eternal. If you are serious and determined to reach the goal of weight management and wealth accumulation, you will see change happen.

How can we measure change? Change comes in many different ways:

- *All-at-once, instant, dramatic, sudden*
- *Starting small, gradual little steps*
- *Consistent and in small increments*

Some resist change and only change when their internal growth becomes too painful to stay the same. It no longer becomes a choice, it becomes a necessity; the only means of survival. The pain is so intense that they release what seems to be all their old habits and choices instantly. Dr. Dean Ornish, author of *Eat More, Weigh Less* states "Comprehensive changes are easier to sustain than moderate ones." For example, it may be easier to stop drinking soda all at once, rather than to cut down gradually. Often we feel the difference immediately, as Ornish states, "Joy is a much more powerful motivator than fear."

Some put off making changes, choosing to take small steps, so they can go through a time of transition. Once we practice the small changes, we feel we can move on to additional transitions with very good results.

Some people change in such small, consistent increments that they are not even aware that change is happening. They go with the flow, continue to challenge themselves, are comfortable with themselves and will stretch and grow. They don't take a lot of risk because they take it slowly, and are open to new ways of thinking and feeling, and growing.

The only thing that stands between you and grand success in living are these two things: Getting started and never quitting!
Dr. Robert Schuller

No matter how you decide to make the change that will lead you through your journey, expect some anxiety, pain and frustration along the way. It will be worth the rewards you will receive at the end of your journey.

Change is not made without inconvenience, even from worse to better.
Samual Johnson

In conclusion

I've found that most of the time individuals seek advice when problems become so bad, they experience fear, despair and extreme pain. I hope that when you've finished *The Weight and Wealth Factors*, you will be equipped with the tools to understanding the why, when, and how you make choices for your health and wealth. Once answered, you will be equipped to implement the strategies in your recipe box.

Success is your destiny. GOOD LUCK!!

Bibliography

Aaberg, Everett. Muscle Mechanics. Dallas: R.I.P.T.
    Publishing, 1998.

Byrne, Robert. The 637 Best Things Anybody Ever Said.
    New York: Anetheum, 1982.

Cibrario, Mark and Stone, Mark. 1999. "F.I.S.T. VideoTape
    Series." 1999.

Goor, Dr. Ron and Nancy. Choose To Lose. Houghton
    Mifflin, January 1999, 3rd Edition.

Fries, Elizabeth, and Croyle, Robert T. "Stereotypes
    Associated with a Low-Fat Diet and Their Relevance to
    Nutrition Education." Journal of the American Dietetic
    Association May 1993, v93.

Kosich, Daniel PhD. "Weight Management Research Update." IDEA Source Nov. - Dec. 1999.

Kravitz, Len, PhD. Lecture: "Current Controversies in Exercise." Fact & Idea Fest. Chicago. June,1999.

Kravitz, Len, PhD. Lecture: "Optimizing Weight Management through Exercise Performance." Fact & Idea Fest. Chicago. June 1999.

Kravitz, Len, PhD. Lecture: "The Physiology of Resistance Training for Women." Fact & Idea Fest. Chicago. June 1999.

Lay, Elizabeth. Thinning From the Inside Out. Bantam Book, 1986.

Letterman, David and the Late Show With David Letterman Writers. David Letterman's Book of Top Ten Lists and Zesty Lo-Cal Chicken Recipes. New York: Bantam Books, 1995.

Livingston, Carole. I'll Never BeFat Again. Barricade Books, Inc., March 1999.

Mellan, Olivia. Money Harmony, Resolving Conflicts in Your Life and Relationships. Walker & Co., February 1995.

Mellin, Laurel, M.A., R.D.. Solution 6 Winning Ways to Permanent Weight Loss. Reganbooks, 1997.

Mueller, Mary Kay. <u>Taking Care of Me, The Habits of Happiness</u>. Mary Kay Mueller, 1996.

Orman, Suze. <u>The 9 Steps To Financial Freedom</u>. Crown Publishing Group, March 1997.

<u>Personal Trainer Certification Manual 2000</u>. New Jersey: American Fitness Professionals & Associates, 1999.

Pond, Jonathan D. CPA with Michael A. Dalton, Ph.D., JD. CFP. CPA and O'Neill Wyss, CFP.. <u>The ABCs of Managing Your Money</u>. NEFE Press.

Pope, Ethan. <u>How To Be A Smart Money Manager.</u> T. Nelson, Nashville, 1995.

Prochnow, Herbert V. & Prochnov, Herbert V. Jr. <u>A Treasure Chest of Quotations for All Occasions.</u> New York: Harper & Row, 1983.

Schwartz, Bob. <u>Diets Do Not Work.</u> Breakthru Publishing, February 1996.

Stuart, Dr. Richard B.. <u>Act Thin, Stay Thin.</u> Norton, New York, 1978.

"The Surgeon General's Report on Nutrition and Health." Washington, D.C.: U.S. Department of Health and Human Services, Public Health Service, DHH (PHS) Publication No. 88-50210, 1988.

Twigg, Stephen. <u>The Kensington Way</u>. Penguin USA, December 1998.

Ungar, Alan B., CFP. <u>Financial Self-Confidence A Women's Guide For The Suddenly Single</u>. Lowell House, 1991

Van Ekeren, Glen. <u>The Speaker's Sourcebook.</u> New Jersey, Prentice-Hall, 1988.

Van Gelder, Naneene & Marks, Sheryl, eds. <u>AerobicDance-Exercise Instructor Manual.</u> San Diego: IDEA Foundation, 1987.

Vest, Herb D. CFP, C, CLU, Niedermeier, Lynn R., CP, CFS. <u>Wealth How To Get It How To Keep It</u>. AMACOM, April 1995.

ANGIE HOLLERICH CEP, CCA, CLL
AREAS OF EXPERTISE

Financial Success: Financial concerns affect your employee's productivity in this time of economic turmoil. Financial education is a vital part of your employee benefits package.

Grab the Brass Ring of Financial Security©
Street Smart Investing (Wall Street, That Is!)©
Making Dollars out of $ense©
Your Earned It...Don't You Want To Keep It?©
Manageable Money Matters©
College Prep: Higher Earning for Higher Learning©
Risk: For Reward Sake©
A Woman's Worth: Your Future Deserves Your Time©
Cents and Sensibility©
The Psychology Of Money©

Financial and health: Every year health care costs increase which affects the bottom line of a company's profit and loss statement. Employees who recognize areas of their health and wealth that need to be addressed become happier and more productive.

The Health and Wealth Factors©
(Can separate and do Health or Wealth separately)
The Inside Skinny to Health and Wealth©

Motivation & Laughter: What motivates you may not be what motivates your employees. A motivated employee is not only happier, but is well rounded and better able to handle unexpected obstacles that pop up in their everyday lives.

Track Your Mood to Train Your Mind©
What if you were Brave?©
Dream, Team, Dare, Care©
Laughter is the Best Medicine©

Communication: Did you know that we process and deliver information differently? A better understanding of our unique communication style will benefit your employee's ability to connect in the office and with your clients and customers.

Brain Power© (As related to: Strategic Communication Skills, Non Traditional Sales)
Leadership, Team Building and Marketing©
Listening and Caring Skills

Sales & Marketing: Sales strategies for industries who can't market and sell in the traditional way.

Non-Traditional Sales Strategies©
How to Succeed in the Financial Industry©
Selling to Women©

*Programs developed for your specific situation and concerns.

Brass Ring Productions Ltd. P. O. Box 307318, Gahanna, Ohio 614-337-2204, fax: 614-337-2283
www.brassringpro.com angieh@brassringpro.com

MARY ZEITLER

Mary Zeitler has worked as a professional educator for 25 years. She received a BS Ed. from Ohio University and an MA Ed. from The Ohio State University. She is an Ace-Certified Group Fitness Instructor and has been leading group fitness for the past 19 years. Mary resides in Westerville, Ohio with her husband, George, and their three children.

Order other publications from Brass Ring Productions!

PLEASE PRINT CLEARLY!

Name _____

Address _____

City/State/Zip _____

Phone _____ E-Mail _____

I would like to receive your e-newsletter   ○ Yes   ○ No

Description	Price	Quantity	Total
The Health & Wealth Factors© Book	$14.95		
The Weight & Wealth Strategy Boxes©			
The Graduate©	$14.95		
Newlyweds©	$14.95		
New Parents©	$14.95		
Suddenly Single©	$14.95		
Retiree©	$14.95		
General©	$14.95		
The Weight & Wealth Factors Journal©	$5.50		
Grab the Brass Ring of Financial Security© Workbook	$19.95		
Grab the Brass Ring of Financial Security© CD	$14.95		
The Wellness Path	$12.95		
Track Your Mood to Change Your Mind©	$ 2.50		
Mission Possible	$15.95		

Order by Fax: Fax this form to 614-337-2283.

Order by Phone: Call 614-337-2204, have your credit card ready, please.

Order by Mail: Mail this form to:
Brass Ring Productions
P.O. Box 307318
Gahanna, Ohio 43230-7318

Subtotal	
Sales Tax add 5.75%	
S & H add $4.50	
TOTAL	

Payment Method

Quantity Discounts Available

Check one: ○ MC   ○ Visa   ○ AMX   ○ Check

Credit Card # _____

Expiration Date _____

Signature _____